# Learning to Read

# Learning to Read
## *Psychology in the Classroom*

*Edited by*
Elaine Funnell
*and*
Morag Stuart

BLACKWELL
Oxford UK & Cambridge USA

Copyright © Blackwell Publishers 1995

First published 1995

Blackwell Publishers Ltd
108 Cowley Road
Oxford   OX4 1JF

Blackwell Publishers Inc.
238 Main Street
Cambridge, Massachusetts 02142
USA

*British Library Cataloguing in Publication Data*
A CIP catalogue record for this book is available from the British Library.

*Library of Congress Cataloging-in-Publication Data*
Learning to read : psychology in the classroom / edited by Elaine
  Funnell and Morag Stuart.
       p.    cm.
  Includes bibliographical references and index.
  ISBN 0–631–19132–1 (acid-free paper). — ISBN 0–631–19133–X
  (pbk. : acid-free paper)
  1. Reading—Congresses.   2. Reading, Psychology of—
Congresses.
  I. Funnell, Elaine.   II. Stuart, Morag.
  LB1050.2.L43   1995
  372.41—dc20                                          94–36183
                                                          CIP

Typeset in 11 on 13 pt Bembo
by Graphicraft Typesetters Ltd, Hong Kong
Printed in Great Britain by Hartnolls Ltd, Bodmin, Cornwall

# Contents

# Contributors

**Roger Beard**, University of Leeds, United Kingdom

**Andrew W. Ellis**, University of York, United Kingdom

**Henryka M. Evans**, University of Dundee, United Kingdom

**Elaine Funnell**, Royal Holloway, University of London, United Kingdom

**Nata Goulandris**, National Hospital's College of Speech Sciences, London, United Kingdom

**Peter J. Hatcher**, University of York, United Kingdom

**Charles Hulme**, University of York, United Kingdom

**Jane Oakhill**, University of Sussex, United Kingdom

**Philip H.K. Seymour**, University of Dundee, United Kingdom

**Margaret Snowling**, University of York, United Kingdom

**Morag Stuart**, Birkbeck College, University of London, United Kingdom

**Nicola Yuill**, University of Sussex, United Kingdom

# *Preface*

## Elaine Funnell and Morag Stuart

The contents of this book started life as a symposium, chaired by Dr Uta Frith and organized by the Cognitive Section of the British Psychological Society at a conference held in London in December 1991. The purpose of the symposium was to present recent experimental evidence on the topic of learning to read to a mixed audience of teachers, educationalists and psychologists, with an emphasis on the relevance of the research to the learning child in the classroom. The conference attracted a large and varied audience who raised many points of interest, so much so that we were encouraged to develop the symposium and publish it as a book.

We, the editors, started out professionally as school teachers, and both in our time puzzled over the mysteries of the processes of learning and teaching reading. While one of us struggled to understand how the small child learns to read and how that learning relates to the teaching received, the other tried to understand how it is that a significant number of children in secondary schools demonstrate that they have failed to learn to read. Later, when we trained as psychologists and began to carry out research into reading processes we looked back, as others have done, to the classroom, and saw the gap between experimental research and the practical world of the school.

When we began to talk to teachers about experimental research in reading we realized that the jargon we used, so familiar to us, was meaningless to teachers and created a barrier to communication.

We also realized that simply telling the teachers about current experimental research was not enough, even though much of it seemed to us to be highly relevant to the classroom. We discovered that the way ahead was to apply the experimental theory to the reading of particular children in the teacher's class; then our approach became meaningful.

In this book, we try as much as we can to follow the same approach. We try to avoid the jargon of psychology, using wherever possible familiar educational terms. Most chapters illustrate points by reporting cases of real children and their revealing comments as they struggle to make sense of print. We try too to examine the reasons why psychology and education do not always communicate as effectively as they should, and we are prepared to admit that the ivory tower approach, together with the fact that research is published in academic journals that are difficult to access, and are often even harder to comprehend, are partly to blame. But there are now a number of very accessible well written books, and we trust that this is the beginning of a trend.

Experimental psychology has at least two aspects to offer to educational practice. First it adds to the understanding of the processes involved in learning to read. Such knowledge should not only guide decisions about methods of teaching beginner readers, but should also add to our understanding of how to help children who fail. Second, the experimental method tests out theories and, by so doing, finds evidence in support of some theories and against others. In this way it can separate fact from fantasy and prevent the adoption of ineffective methods *before* they reach the classroom. Not surprisingly then, a central theme of this book is the place of the experimental method in the study of reading development.

The book of course belongs to the contributors of the chapters, to whom we are greatly indebted. Each has a distinguished academic record, either as an educationalist in the field of reading development or as an experimental psychologist trying to understand how children learn to read and why reading development sometimes fails. They write with authority.

The book is intended for teachers, particularly those in training, educationalists, psychologists, and anyone interested in the study of how children learn to read. We hope you will all find the book useful.

1 ————————————————————————

# Learning to Read: Psychology and Education

Roger Beard

————————————————————————

*Roger Beard is an educationalist. He looks at the contribution that psychology can make to the teaching of reading. Educational practice is based upon theory, and it is the theory of the teaching of reading with which he is concerned.*

*He begins with a review of the theories of teaching reading which are currently influential – the real books approach, the apprenticeship approach, the psycholinguistic guessing game approach – and provides evidence that these play a central role in teacher education. The historical background to these approaches is detailed and the reason why these theories may have evolved is explained. While he is careful to point out the positive aspects of these approaches, he notes that a significant number of publications have raised doubts about the efficacy of the approaches and that, to date, these doubts have largely been overlooked. He is concerned that the theories have received such widespread acceptance, and reveals their obvious shortcomings by systematically presenting evidence from a range of sources, including experimental psychological research. While he is critical of the educationalists for accepting theoretical approaches uncritically, he is equally critical of psychologists for failing, on the whole, to make their work accessible to educationalists, and suggests that the ability to write in tune with the thinking of teachers and educationalists has been a factor in the influence of educational theories and the neglect of relevant psychological evidence.*

## Does Teacher Training Neglect Psychological Research?

The focus of this chapter is on a curious paradox in the study and teaching of reading. Of all the relevant disciplines, psychology ought to have as much, if not more, to offer teacher education as any other. Yet it seems to be one of the least influential disciplines in initial and in-service courses and in creating the theories on which these courses draw. This might not be such a bad thing if the theories which were influential were entirely sound and reflected the findings from recent psychological research. But this is not always the case. Books and courses in teacher education are influenced by a variety of ideas which often seem to be at odds with research findings and which are sometimes summarized in unsatisfactory slogans. Examples include the following assumptions:

1  that the processes of literacy learning are very similar to those involved in learning the mother tongue (a 'whole language' point of view);
2  that literacy learning is natural and 'emerges' from meaningful experiences with print;
3  that 'phonics' plays only a small part in reading, which is more a process of predicting meanings and checking them out, particularly by using first letter cues;
4  that only 'real books' (i.e. those which are not part of a reading scheme) make 'real readers'.

The widespread influence of such views in teacher education was noted after a survey of recommended books in public sector (i.e. college and polytechnic) initial teacher training courses on reading in England and Wales in 1989.[1] Tom Gorman, who directed the survey for the National Foundation of Educational Research (NFER), noted that the majority of the books in the lists espoused an approach to the teaching of reading which was by then sufficiently widely accepted to be considered 'orthodox'. This comprised a view of reading sometimes referred to as the 'apprenticeship approach', which deals not only (reasonably) with 'shared reading' but also (more radically) with the kinds of ideas set out above. In a subsequent study of reading lists in initial teacher education in England and Wales, also by the NFER,[2] the booklet which sets out the 'apprenticeship approach' was found to be the most recommended book.[3]

This chapter will suggest ways in which the findings from psychological research can provide more balanced insights for use in teacher education and can counter some of the misleading ideas which have become influential in recent years. It will end with some suggestions on how such findings might be more widely used in teacher education.

I should add that the new 'orthodoxy', to which Tom Gorman referred, has apparently not been so influential in schools. There are few indications that practices have been widely influenced by the kinds of ideas listed above. I would also like to stress that, as a primary teacher and teacher trainer, I do not speak as a specialist psychologist and my eclectic approach is reflected in my own publications.[4]

In order to investigate this complex area, it is necessary to trace how the radical ideas in the current orthodoxy have been influenced by 'psycholinguistic' theories of the 1970s and how these theories were in turn a reaction against the 'drills and skills' teaching approaches which were associated with behavioural psychology and structural linguistics, especially in the United States. From this brief historical review of 'reaction and over-reaction', we can better consider how we can draw upon recent work in the 'psychology of reading' while also retaining the most helpful of the radical ideas which are currently so influential, at least in teacher education.

It also has to be noted that there has sometimes been an apparent hostility towards psychologists and psychology in literacy courses in teacher education,[5] which seems not so apparent in educational studies courses. There is also the suspicion that findings from psychological research have been side-lined because they do not appear to confirm the radical theories which have been so influential.

## Other Influential Theories in Teacher Education

In place of psychology, dominant theories of reading in teacher education seem to be drawn from literary, ethnographic and certain 'psycholinguistic' points of view. Before I discuss what psychology can offer current reading studies in teacher education, it may be helpful briefly to note the positive features and limitations of these other influences in teacher education.

There is now a major interest in the use of books in the teaching of reading which fulfil a variety of demanding literary criteria. The Cox Report, from the National Curriculum English Working Group,[6] caught the mood in its suggestions that books selected for young children should have bold, easily read print, well-matched illustrations which enhance the text and stories which are capable of interpretation at a number of levels and, most importantly, they should be books which children enjoy.

In an age when children are bombarded with visual media, it seems particularly prudent to draw upon literary criteria in selecting books which compare favourably with other attractions. I have suggested in my own book, *Developing Reading 3–13*,[7] that we are in the midst of a golden age of picture books, which has undoubtedly informed thinking on the design of reading schemes as well. In the light of these well-founded developments, the criticism of the use of the so-called 'real books' in the teaching of reading seems misguided, such is the quality of the work of their authors and illustrators. Problems can be envisaged, though, if the suggestion that these books can 'teach' reading is taken too literally and if well-meaning teachers use only non-scheme books and an informal, 'shared reading' approach. Barbara Tizard's[8] research in inner city schools and survey reports by Her Majesty's Inspectors (HMI)[9] provide some cautionary evidence in this respect.

Tizard warns, from the findings of a three-year study of thirty-three schools, that 'simply introducing children to books in a happy atmosphere does not ensure that they will make a connection between meaning and print, or have an understanding of written language'.[10] In 1991, HMI noted, from a study of 120 schools, that exclusive 'real book' approaches run the risk of giving too little attention to the systematic teaching of skills for tackling print.[11]

It may also be misguided to dismiss reading schemes in principle, partly because they too have improved in design and content in recent years and partly because they can provide a *continuing context* (i.e. across and between books) to support children in the early stages of learning to read. Katharine Perera provides some very interesting findings on this issue. In examining samples of reading scheme and 'individual' books in terms of their rhythm, story structure, grammar and vocabulary, she found no clear distinctions between the two kinds of books. Good and less effective writing was found in schemes and individual books alike.[12]

One of the most influential critics of reading schemes has been Margaret Meek, who has criticized 'reading experts' for 'decontextualizing' reading in order to describe it and has gone on to develop the argument that 'only real books make real readers'.[13]

Few people would deny the role which good individual books can play in reading development, but it seems to be a mistake implicitly to condemn all books which have been deliberately written to teach reading as part of a 'package' of materials. Anyone seeking the research underpinning this argument will note Meek's admission that any significant reading research she has done rests on her having treated anecdotes as evidence.[14] This contrast with the more scientific traditions of psychological reading research needs to be borne in mind in relation to an associated research project, in which 'real books' were used to meet the needs of adolescent non-readers (or 'inexperienced' readers). A careful reading of the resulting book, *Achieving Literacy* (p. 223), reveals that the project was, in fact, inconclusive. Thus, even after 'contextualizing' the study of the reading of these young people and using anecdotes as evidence, the investigators could only conclude that they were 'too late'.[15]

Reading studies in teacher education have also been increasingly influenced by ethnographic approaches, which have adopted anthropological methods of trying to describe events and situations from the point of view of those being studied. Such approaches have been especially influential in the development of interest in 'emergent literacy', although the term was coined by a psychologist, Marie Clay.[16] In fact Clay's original use of the term 'emergent' literacy, to indicate 'partly formed' literacy, seems to have been revised to include more radical ideas by subsequent writers. In this revised view, literacy development is seen as a natural response to purposeful literacy environments; children's attempts to make marks and to create meanings by guessing at the content of attractive picture books may be seen as 'literacy events'.[17] There is no clear demarcation between the literacy learning of the pre-school years and the early years at school; terms like 'pre-reading' and 'reading readiness' are avoided. Unfortunately, though, books on emergent literacy do not always explain when and why scribbles and guesses at print cease to be features of emergent literacy and instead become indications of the need for some kind of intervention.[18]

Again, few would deny that ethnographic data can enrich social research, but providing 'natural descriptions' of children's literacy learning in a valid and reliable way is not as straightforward as is sometimes assumed. As Lawrence Stenhouse once said, 'there is no telling it "as it is"'.[19] The very way in which we define and interpret children's 'literacy acts' demands interpretation in itself. The significance of scribbles, invented spellings and guesses at the meaning of print is not necessarily self-evident. Attempts to explain this significance may conceivably refer to behaviour and comprehension which eventually prove to be inefficient and inappropriate, even as approximations, and which the children may themselves in time disown. It is not always acknowledged that ethnographic studies require the 'triangulation' of other sources of interpretation and the use of other sources of evidence to avoid the pitfalls of romantic theorizing from what is observed.[20]

## Psycholinguistics and Psychology

In order to explain the origins of the orthodoxy to which Tom Gorman referred, it is necessary to go back to what can be generally described as the Smith–Goodman 'psycholinguistic' model of the fluent reading process, which became increasingly influential from the early 1970s onwards. Many publications follow David Crystal's definition of 'psycholinguistics' as the study of language variation in relation to thinking and to other psychological processes within the individual.[21] Kenneth Goodman and Frank Smith, however, have given the term a more radical connotation in reading studies. In this view of reading, anticipation and prediction are emphasized rather than accurate decoding of texts. Kenneth Goodman's notion of reading being a 'psycholinguistic guessing game' has become very well known and in recent years he has promoted a 'whole language' approach which draws close parallels between the development of spoken and written language.[22] The most influential work of Frank Smith has included his nine rules for the teaching of reading that teachers would do well NOT to follow: e.g. (1) aiming for an early mastery of the rules of reading; (2) ensuring that phonic skills are learned and used; (3) teaching letters or words one at a time, making sure each is learned before moving on; (4) making word-perfect reading a prime objective.[23] Similarly, Smith's attack on 'the fallacy of phonics' has probably shaken the confidence of large numbers of teachers in drawing children's attention to sound–letter relationships, perhaps especially teachers joining the profession. Smith and Goodman base their persuasive arguments on accounts of what they claim to be the nature of the fluent reading process and, in order to understand the radical edge to these theories, we must look back beyond them to the orthodoxies which they in turn replaced.

The middle years of the twentieth century saw psychology being dominated by behaviourism, in which conduct and stimuli are systematically studied, rather than subjective experience and introspection. The great appeal of behaviourism was that it seemed more 'scientific' than other perspectives.[24] This was also true of Leonard Bloomfield's work in 'structural' linguistics[25] which concentrated on analysing sentences into their constituent parts and which approached the study of meaning in a very narrow way. Goodman and Smith must have been aware that these theories could have a very unsatisfactory influence on teaching practices and on the design of teaching materials, which could be misleadingly narrow and insufficiently sensitive to how language was used to generate meaning. Their radical alternative seemed to be in line with the implications of the seminal work of Noam Chomsky who had shown how human language acquisition could not be explained by a 'linear' model.[26] Children did not just learn language by imitation or by connecting together various bits of language (e.g. sounds, words or phrases). Using their inherited capacity for language learning (a kind of 'language acquisition device') children all over the world seemed to learn to speak by a process of hypothesis-testing and discovery, through authentic interaction with others.

It seemed a small jump to apply the same model of learning to reading, even though Chomsky was far more cautious in what he said on literacy. But by 1971 Frank Smith was sewing the seeds of what was to become the 'whole language' movement by suggesting that precisely the same kind of argument may be applied to reading – that basically a child is equipped with every skill that he or she needs in order to read and to learn to read.[27] As Marilyn Jager Adams has subsequently pointed out, Smith concluded that, given adequate and motivating experience with meaningful text, learning to read should be as natural as learning to talk. Adams acknowledges that Smith's argument was, in some respects, insightful: he conceded that phonic analysis helped the reader to mediate the identification of words that cannot be identified on sight. He was also correct in arguing that skilful reading could not proceed on the basis of identifying one letter – or word – at a time. But extending the ideas about the language acquisition device, the details of which were only speculative, was, according to Adams, an enormous and gratuitous leap.[28]

## Critiques of Kenneth Goodman's Theories

Let us first look at the influences and critiques of the work of Kenneth Goodman. In his publications at the end of the 1960s, Goodman argued that there was a close and direct parallel between the learning of spoken and written language. He asserted that learning to read was as natural as learning to speak. In his celebrated (some would say notorious) 1967 paper, in which he wrote that reading ought to be seen as a 'psycholinguistic guessing game', he suggested that the basis of fluent reading was not word recognition but hypothesis-forming about the meanings which 'lie ahead' and the selection of maximally 'productive' cues to confirm or deny these meanings.

There was no shortage of critical responses to this view of fluent reading but, like the critiques of Frank Smith's theories, they were far less influential. Eleanor Gibson and Harry Levin pointed out that Goodman's model of reading does not explain how the reader knows when to confirm guesses and where to look to do so.[29] Philip Gough has consistently challenged how predictable language is.[30] His studies suggest that, at most, we can only predict one word in four when all the succeeding text is covered. (As you read the rest of my chapter, try this for yourself.) And the words which we can most easily predict are the ones we can most easily recognize, anyway. In fact, there is a curious contradiction in these 'psycholinguistic' theories of fluent reading. They are inspired by Chomsky's work on the 'generative' qualities of language (even small children are capable of saying things they have never heard before). Yet these theories stress the 'predictability' of language use. If language use is so open-ended and essentially unpredictable, then, as Jessie Reid has pointed out, these 'psycholinguistic' theories of reading are at odds with their own roots.[31]

Jessie Reid has in fact provided one of the most searching critiques of Goodman's theories. She notes how confusing Goodman is in the way he oscillates between the terms 'predicting', 'anticipating', 'expecting' and 'guessing' which, although closely related, are not synonymous. She asks a number of important questions: How does the reader know which cues will be most productive? Are the criteria fixed for any given word? If the predicted word is not on the page, what then? Can readers sample for the 'most productive cues' in a word they did not expect? Most fundamentally, is the guessing game model optimally efficient?

## Critiques of Frank Smith's Theories

There were similar critiques of Frank Smith's arguments right through the 1970s and 1980s, but for some reason these critical responses have not seemed to have been widely taken up, especially in many influential publications in British teacher education. Joyce Morris has pointed out the lack of evidence for Smith's argument that meaning precedes decoding and for the conclusion that print can be directly converted to meaning, especially in a writing system which is itself *alphabetic*, in which the symbols used in written English (alphabet letters and groups of letters) were designed by the early scribes to represent the speech sounds (phonemes) of English.[32] In this light, Smith is in danger of implying that reading should be taught by treating written English like a 'logographic' system in which each symbol represents a word.

Another searching criticism of Smith's theories comes from the linguist Katharine Perera.[33] In a review of his 1978 book, *Reading*, in which Smith re-worked much of the material of his earlier books, she shows how he over-states his case at several points of his argument and how his cavalier-like writing contains several important errors (e.g. that children can remember the look of a word as easily as a human face). She argues that, in any case, studies of fluent reading do not necessarily indicate how children should be taught and that phonological processing (the perception and manipulation of speech sounds) plays a greater role in early reading than Smith suggests. His conclusions about the importance of guessing from context are based, Perera reminds us, on experiments with adults in which the texts are made deliberately difficult and she concludes that the book is not sound enough to be used as a handbook by the teachers of reading for whom it was written.

The response of Denis Stott to Smith's arguments and influence was to decry the 'psycholinguistic invasion' and to warn of the '"progressive" pressure to decry systematic teaching' which was associated with the growing influence of Smith and Goodman.[34] In a sharply worded attack on Frank Smith's views in particular, Stott warns that it is misleading to compare the learning of speech by 'immersion' in meaningful contexts with the learning of reading by immersion in environmental print because the former is inescapable for young children whereas the latter is dispensable. He anticipates the later research findings of Linnea Ehri,[35] who reports that when young children appear to read environmental print, they may in fact be 'reading the context' and may not be able to recognize the same word or phrase when it is encountered elsewhere, perhaps with a different typeface or logo. Stott is unhappy about the way Smith disparages teaching about system, technique and method and points out the unreliability of context cues, on which Goodman's 'psycholinguistic guessing game model of reading rests', unless children are also encouraged to give detailed attention to the spelling patterns of words. Stott argues that it is misleading to caricature phonics teaching as drills and laborious sounding out. He stresses that phonics should be seen as a kind of 'guided induction'. This indication will help children to respond to sounds in words and relate these variations in sound to a sequence of symbols. Stott notes that academics who should have known better had fallen into unrealistic dogmatism. Rather prophetically, Stott warns that uncritical acceptance of these misleading 'psycholinguistic' ideas could be ideologically convenient to those who would like to dispense with teacher education in the institutional (i.e. higher education) sense.

Psychological research has also consistently indicated that contextual cues play a less central role in fluent reading than has been assumed by Smith and Goodman. In the United States of America, these studies were brought together by Keith Stanovich in a long review paper which explored the debate between 'bottom-up' and 'top-down' theories of reading development. In the former, reading is assumed to develop in a series of discrete stages of information processing.[36] In the latter, reading is seen as the sampling of textual information in order to test hypotheses. Stanovich argues that fluent reading is an interactive process in which information is used from several knowledge sources simultaneously (letter recognition, letter–sound relationships, vocabulary, knowledge of syntax and meaning). In contrast to the top-down theories which have become so prevalent in teacher education, he shows that good readers do not use context cues more than poor readers. In contrast, it is *weaknesses* in word recognition that lead to relatively greater use of contextual cues as reading proficiency of continuous text develops. Better readers may appear to use context cues more effectively in cloze procedure activities when words are artificially deleted and the *surrounding text is visible*. But what is at issue here is not the presence of contextual knowledge in good readers, but their use of and reliance upon it in normal reading of continuous text. Good readers may be more sensitive to context, and yet less dependent upon it, because information is more easily available to them from other sources.

This conclusion flies in the face of the top-down views of reading of Smith and Goodman, in which it was assumed that fluent readers relied less on graphic cues as their prediction skills and hypothesis-making capacities became more sophisticated. Instead, Stanovich draws on dozens of studies to show that fluent readers are distinguished by rapid word recognition and effective comprehension strategies.

In the United Kingdom, a similarly extensive review has been brought together by Jane Oakhill and Alan Garnham.[37] Like Stanovich, they question top-down theories in the light of the relative speeds of the processes involved. They show how, in fluent reading, the use of contextual cues to help identify a word is usually unnecessary because words are recognized from visual information so quickly. Oakhill and Garnham also review the research which indicates that a small but substantial number of children have specific reading comprehension difficulties, even though they are able to decode words reasonable efficiently.

Thus, by the end of the 1980s, many aspects of Goodman's and Smith's theories were looking decidedly threadbare. Yet they appear undaunted by recurrent criticism. In a recent book, sardonically titled *Phonics Phacts*, Goodman re-asserts the 'natural' view of learning to read.[38] In responding to the many research studies reviewed in Marilyn Jager Adams's *Beginning to Read* which seem to undermine his arguments, he argues that his is a 'real world' (as opposed to an 'instructional and laboratory studies' view) although, unconvincingly, he relies for evidence on experiments with short, decontextualized and disfigured texts (i.e. not from the 'real world') in support of his case.

Frank Smith must also have raised many eyebrows when he began the fourth edition of his book *Understanding Reading* with a blanket repudiation of the more recent research that has proved inconsistent with his original insights. It was perhaps this inflexibility which prompted Marilyn Jager Adams to launch her own direct attack on Smith's theories in 1991.[39]

## Insights into Reading from Marilyn Jager Adams

Adams examines several of Smith's assertions in the light of recent psychological research and shows how misleading they can be for teachers.

'Skilful readers do not attend to individual words of text'(?)

Referring to research involving computer-mediated eye movement technology, Adams confirms that fluent readers do skip a few words, mostly short function words, but that most words are processed either in eye fixations or in the peripheral vision of the saccades of eye movements. Adams feels that Smith is right in warning against an over-concentration on individual words, but wrong to imply that readers should not process them. Skilful readers have learned to process words and spellings very quickly but such automaticity comes from having read words, not from skipping them.

'Skilful readers don't process individual letters'(?)

Adams acknowledges that skilful readers do not look or feel as if they are processing individual letters of text as they read, but research has repeatedly shown that they do, in a process of 'parallel processing'. Individual letters and spelling patterns are processed interdependently as the text is perceived and comprehended. To deny letter identification in reading is like saying that there is no such thing as a grain of sand. Skilled readers can process letters so quickly because of visual knowledge of words. This knowledge is based on their memories of the sequences of letters which make up words. The more we read, the more this knowledge is reinforced and enriched.

'Spelling–sound translations are irrelevant for readers'(?)

Adams replies that skilful readers do automatically and irrepressibly translate print to speech while they read. Many words become so well learned that they are quickly recognized as wholes. This learning may be helped by the fact that most frequently used words are short in spelling and sound. But the information in a text depends disproportionately on its less familiar words. This constraint undermines Smith's assumption that children can depend on the meaning of a text to infer the meaning of its less familiar words. The habit of sounding out words becomes invaluable for infrequent words (infection . . . penicillin . . . discovered . . . Alexander Fleming . . . antibiotics) and even for wholly unfamiliar words (hypermetropical . . . hackmatack . . . thigmotaxis). As children's reading develops, the speech system ensures that words which are known but which are visually unfamiliar are recognized quickly and without the loss of reading speed which impedes comprehension.

'Don't teach children about spellings and sounds'(?)

Adams points out that this stricture reflects three of Smith's insights: (a) that spelling to sound translations are unnecessary; (b) that children will discover the distinctive features of writing easily from exposure to meaningful print; and (c) that fluent readers sample across whole meaningful chunks of text rather than individual letters and words.

Adams concludes that Smith is actually wrong on all three counts. She reminds us that a knowledge of spelling–sound relations enables children to lock in to the visual sequence of printed letters so that it supports learning about the spelling system. Children have to learn about the arbitrary symbols which are the letters of the alphabet. Children have to learn to be consciously aware of the phonemes on which our alphabetic writing system is based. Children may be helped to become aware of syllables and rhymes and alliteration before the more demanding task of distinguishing between phonemes. In all this, Adams stresses the importance of teaching about spellings and sounds in the context of reading and writing experiences which engage and motivate children.

## The 'Psycholinguistic' Influence on the 'Apprenticeship Approach'

Critiques such as these reveal how misleading it can be to base educational provision on many of the arguments which can be found in the writing of Kenneth Goodman and Frank Smith. Yet, perhaps because these arguments were plausible and ideologically appealing, it was the publications by Smith and Goodman which inspired the cult ideas of the 1980s. Prominent among these ideas were those which were central to the most recommended source on reading in initial teacher education, a booklet on the 'apprenticeship approach' by a teacher in an infant school.[40]

As was noted earlier, the booklet deals with the shared reading teaching method. In principle, it can be used with any kind of book but, in its original form, it is an integrated part of the use of 'real books'. The effectiveness of the approach has not apparently been systematically studied in detail, although a feature article in the *Times Educational Supplement* quoted the head teacher of the adjacent junior school suggesting that the apprenticeship approach seemed to promote interest in books but not necessarily the word attack skills which children need for independent reading.[41]

It is interesting to note how the theory of the apprenticeship approach has been derived from several writers whose work has already been referred to: Kenneth Goodman, Margaret Meek and Frank Smith feature in the references, although the main and laudable concern is that, in the past, children have learned to read, but have not become 'readers' in the second sense of developing a life-long love of the pleasures to be derived from reading. This is attributed to the poor quality of early reading experiences, over-concentration on sub-skills and a relative neglect of meaning and 'meaningful' reading experiences in early childhood education. These arguments have clearly struck a chord, because the author writes in the second edition of having given talks to thousands of teachers after the booklet was published in 1985. It may have influenced the first version of the National Curriculum, too, as shared reading was the only teaching approach directly referred to in the Non-Statutory Guidance for English.[42]

Actually, it is debatable whether 'apprenticeship' is an appropriate term for learning to read. Its theory refers to a parallel with engineering apprentices who, it is suggested, learn by 'sitting with Nelly'. However, information from the husband of an eminent psychologist, himself an engineer, throws doubt on this. Discrepancies between the two learning contexts include the following: in the early stages of an engineering apprenticeship, apprentices may practise on material that is not part of a 'real' job (this can involve using scrap material); when engineering apprentices move on to work which is part of a 'real job', the activities are closely matched to the apprentices' ability, being graded in difficulty and comprising very small components of larger operations; contacts between skilled worker and apprentice are very brief and concern just the jobs to be done at the time (practice and repetition are very important). In engineering at least, the idea that apprentices will 'sit and watch' and eventually join in everything seems to be an inaccurate one.[43]

## More Questions about the Apprenticeship Approach

As well as these questions about the term itself and the lack of evidence on its effectiveness, there is little in the apprenticeship approach to explain *how* children learn to read by its use. Instead there are lists of 'reading behaviours' to describe when an adult reads the text, when a child reads a 'known text' and when a child reads an 'unknown text'.

There is little in the way of 'fall-back' for the child who does not make progress, although there is obvious concern for supportive teaching contexts and meaningful texts. Nevertheless, it is not clear what the apprenticeship approach assumes about the way children learn the written language system, and similar questions can be asked of its assumptions compared with those which were asked of the 'psycholinguistic' views of reading which were mentioned earlier. Does the apprenticeship approach treat written English as a 'logographic' system in which each new word is learned separately? Does it assume that the spelling patterns are so difficult to teach that we have to leave them for the children to learn? Does it assume that context cues are so 'directive' that word recognition is largely a matter of confirming expectations? (If so, where do the context cues come from, if not from other words?) Or does it assume the use of other teaching materials and approaches which are not mentioned in the booklet?

## A New Orthodoxy?

As was noted at the beginning of this chapter, the influence of the 'apprenticeship approach' in initial teacher training courses is indicated by surveys carried out by the NFER. In the first of these reports, Tom Gorman notes that the assumptions underlying the approach are clearly indicated in its 'central propositions'.

1 *'In many ways the acquisition of written language is comparable to that of spoken language.'* (Significantly, the words of Frank Smith are cited in support, that learning to read involves no learning ability that children have not already been called upon to exercise in order to understand the language spoken at home.)
2 *'Essentially reading cannot be taught in a formal, sequenced way any more than speech can be.'*
3 *'Reading is not a series of small skills fluently used; it is a process of getting meaning.'*
4 *'The text offered to the child is crucially important.'* The theory is elaborated to argue that the logical challenge to the teacher is to provide such a wide range of 'real books' that the children will find their own book which will be meaningful to them; letting them choose which ones they wish to read and letting them find the meaning for themselves.
5 *The role of the adult as a guiding friend.*[44]

Recently these propositions have been examined in detail by Jane Oakhill and myself.[45] Having written a critique of the apprenticeship approach, we would agree with Tom Gorman that it embodies many insights, but that it does not necessarily require teachers to be equipped with the knowledge they need to think analytically about the language of their pupils or of the texts they are exposed to. It tends to underplay the amount of knowledge teachers need to have about the sound system and the written system of English in order to be able to intervene strategically to assist children to understand the relationships between these. He goes on to provide a clear warning, which could serve as an incentive to all psychologists who are concerned with current influences on literacy teaching and learning:

It is easy for teachers in training, the majority of whom have no more than a preliminary exposure to theories and practices of language description, to misunderstand and to misapply the principles underlying the apprenticeship approach, all of which are open to question and misinterpretation. This point applies in particular to the principles that concern the relationship of written and spoken English.[46]

## Uncertainties about the Transfer of Learning

Perhaps the most evident weakness which is linked to the Smith–Goodman legacy is that the apprenticeship approach does not make it clear how children *transfer* their learning from one book to another, or even what they learn which is transferable.

The issue of the transfer of learning is a central one because of the way the apprenticeship approach has been coupled to the use of non-scheme books which, by their very nature, are not linked in any way in vocabulary, grammatical pattern or organization. The recent research by Katharine Perera, into various features of reading scheme and individual books, has shown what a huge learning load this can place on children.[47] Ironically, the theory of the apprenticeship approach touches upon this issue in a reference to reading scheme books: there is criticism of books where there is no connection between each unit and where the next word is quite arbitrary within wide limits; the theory notes that what meaning there is has to be imposed upon the text.[48] It does not seem to be recognized that the issue of supportive continuity is of similar importance between books as well as between words. The apprenticeship approach provides support by reading to the children any words which they do not recognize, but it is unclear how independent reading can be promoted if repeated sharing of a book is not accompanied by other types of teaching.

## Vygotsky and Reading

Just as the notion of apprenticeship in reading can be questioned, so too can the use made of Lev Vygotsky's work. While the apprenticeship approach makes just passing reference, it has been sometimes suggested that it represents an application of Vygotsky's framework of collaborative learning which appears in *Mind in*

*Society*.[49] However, Vygotsky's suggestions are easier to apply to the solving of practical problems such as those cited by Derek Edwards and Neil Mercer[50] in craft, science or information technology. His more specific consideration of literacy was included in *Thought and Language*, in which he argued that 'Written speech is a separate linguistic function, differing from oral speech in both structure and mode of functioning.'[51] Several researchers have adapted such an argument in various types of 'language awareness' theory.[52] These are concerned with the ways in which learners can be helped to attend to how the structure of spoken language maps onto that of written language, a point which will be taken up again in the conclusion to this chapter.

## The Question of 'Phonics'

In keeping with the 'psycholinguistic' influence, phonics is treated almost as anathema in the apprenticeship approach. It refers to phonics in terms of it being a 'dreaded subject' and suggests that phonics is only one 'very small part' of reading.[53] The approach seems to overlook the fact that the basis of the English writing system (its orthography) is the representation of its speech sounds (its phonology) by alphabet letters. It is not surprising, then, that there is in fact a vast amount of evidence from psychological research to suggest that children's 'phonological awareness' is associated with success in early independent reading.[54] As will be seen below, this success seems to be especially linked to the use of entertaining texts such as rhyming verse and other forms of 'word play'. While some phonological awareness is likely to come indirectly from shared reading, research suggests that many children are likely to benefit from being encouraged *systematically* to attend to the spelling patterns of English and the speech sounds to which they relate.

There is a concession in the apprenticeship approach[55] that children will need to learn the basic sounds of the alphabet in their usual initial letter forms and combinations. This emphasis on initial letters may be a reflection of the assumptions that fluent reading is essentially a matter of prediction but, as was pointed out earlier, this view has now been discredited. Given the alphabetic nature of written English, which encompasses every part of every word and comprises a representation of approximately forty-four phonemes by letters and groups of letters (e.g. vowel and consonant digraphs), then this aspect of the apprenticeship approach appears to be based not only on partial information but on a misleading view of English orthography.

It is likely that the apprenticeship approach is unduly influenced by Frank Smith's argument that there are over two hundred correspondences between letters and sounds, even in short, 'easy' words in written English.[56] However, as several researchers have pointed out, this kind of analysis does not take account of the patterns created by relationships between morphemes, the units of meaning within words (e.g. reading the two sound–letter relationships represented by the second 'vowel sounds' in photograph and photography is helped by their shared morpheme). Similarly, such discussion needs to take account of the 'serial probability' of the English spelling system. One group of letters in the first part of a word is far more likely to be followed by some groups than others: 'r' at the beginning of a word will normally be followed by a vowel and pronounced /r/. But when 'r' follows a vowel, it will probably be part of a vowel digraph (e.g. 'farm', 'firm', 'form'). The main exception to this is when 'r' follows a vowel at a morpheme boundary, where a hyphen may be used (e.g. 're-run'). The influence of morphemes is one of a number of such 'qualifications' in the way the sound–letter system operates in English, making it, according to Kenneth Albrow, a 'system of systems'.[57] Furthermore, if written English is instead treated as a 'whole word' or 'logographic' system in order to make the teaching of reading more 'meaningful', then learners are confronted, in principle, not with hundreds of sound–letter relationships but with *thousands* of different whole word 'characters'.


## Psychology and the 'New Phonics'


This leads on to where recent work in psychology has broadened and clarified the role of phonics or, more specifically, phonological processing in reading development. This work does not imply a 'phonics first and fast' approach, as is sometimes assumed. Indeed, studies of how children learn to distinguish and manipulate phonemes indicate that experience of reading continuous text has a very important role to play. But word making and breaking can help reading development too, especially in helping children to split syllables into their alliterative and rhyming parts (e.g. h/op, h/oop, h/it; or h/op, p/op, t/op). In the United Kingdom, Usha Goswami is undertaking research at Cambridge University on how children learn to read by making analogies between groups of alphabet letters. This research promises to have far-reaching implications for the teaching of reading.[58]

In *Beginning to Read*, Marilyn Jager Adams (1990) gives an indication of how children's phonological development can be fostered by a range of increasingly demanding activities which are derived from psychological research. First of all, she stresses a number of 'prerequisites', including the range and quality of children's pre-school experiences in literacy and the range and quality of books which are used in the teaching of reading. She also makes important assumptions about teachers' professional knowledge in dealing with the English writing system and the role of sound–letter relationships within it.

Adams then goes on to outline how aspects of the following sequence can help develop children's awareness and knowledge, according to their perceived needs:[59]

1  becoming aware of syllables in rhythmical texts, perhaps by clapping along with them;
2  becoming aware of the different sounds in words, perhaps by 'odd one out' games, e.g. '*h*ill, pat, *h*op; or h*o*p, l*o*t, gun';
3  being encouraged to 'blend' words, to help children develop a sense of phonemes, as well as familiarity with and a memory for phonemes;
4  being encouraged to 'break sounds' off, by splitting syllables, e.g. h/op, into other words with the same onset, 'h—' (alliteration), or with the same rime, '—op';
5  being helped to detect all the sounds in a word and to 'segment' them, e.g. /h/o/p/ (perhaps using counters to 'record' the sounds if necessary);

6   being able to change the order of sounds in words, e.g. taking
    the 'o' from 'hop' and putting in 'i'; saying 'hill' without the
    'h'; or adding 'h' to the beginning of 'ill'.

As was said above, it is important to bear in mind that many
children will be developing this awareness and knowledge as an
integral part of their reading of continuous text. Indeed being able
to 'change the order of sounds in words' above seems to be closely
linked with increased fluency in reading. But, as Adams convincingly shows, a working knowledge of the structure of words is of
enormous importance in being able to read the unfamiliar words
of different subject areas for which 'contextual cues' are often too
vague.

## Conclusion

So, what can be done to make more of psychology in the study
and teaching of reading? Readers of this chapter will have their
own responses to the ground I have covered, but here are my
own. As befits an eclectic educationalist, I shall make reference
not only to psychology but to other academic disciplines on which
literacy studies can draw.

### Research findings need to be shared more widely

Anyone who makes a thorough study of this area is likely to feel
uneasy that the current orthodoxy seems to be a misinformed
one. Literacy learning may need to be seen rather differently from
the ways in which some 'psycholinguistic' publications and the
'apprenticeship approach' have defined it. The first version of
the National Curriculum in English seemed to be caught up in the
prevailing *zeitgeist*: 'phonic cues' were coyly only mentioned once,
and then in a way which seemed to equate them with picture
cues. We may need new theories which help to bring us back to
the nature of the print on the page. While it is obviously important to encourage children actively to construct meanings from

texts, it is also important to recognize the role of efficient word recognition in this, rather than prediction and checking, plausible though this idea may seem. We obviously read with a variety of *'expectancies'*, but fluent reading seems to depend on fast recognition of words and groups of letters far more than some influential theories have acknowledged. It may be more realistic to see written language as largely *un*predictable and to recognize that this is what provides its endless novelty and reward.

It needs to be more widely recognized that written English is essentially an alphabetic system, a representation of speech sounds by alphabet letters. It is hardly surprising, then, that systematic teaching of how this system works is helpful to many children in the context of their experience of informative and entertaining books.[60,61] It is also hardly surprising that young children draw intuitively on the alphabetic system when attempting to spell words.[62]

Numerous findings from psychological research have cast doubt on the influential 'psycholinguistic' and 'apprenticeship' theories. It is unfortunate that some of the insights provided by the 'New Literacy studies', in which sociological perspectives are very much in evidence, seem to be taking these theories for granted and treating them in an uncritical way.[63] Teacher training in particular will benefit from a wider use of sources which also pull together what might be called the 'New Psychology studies', including what are sometimes called the 'new phonics'. A recent example of such a book is the summary of *Beginning to Read* by Marilyn Jager Adams.[64]

## Psychologists need to write more accessibly

But *Beginning to Read* may be some way from fulfilling this role. It is written by a group from the University of Illinois and it lacks some of the spark of Marilyn Adams's original writing. It may also be too academic for a more popular take-up. The engaging, non-technical style of Frank Smith's *Reading* may be one reason for this book's success, even if some of his central arguments were wrong. Although this present chapter is written primarily for teachers, it is important to note that it has implications for psychologists, too. The challenge for psychologists is to find avenues for writing responsibly and informatively about reading in a more reader-friendly way than is generally their custom, without betraying the caution which befits scientific endeavour. Peter Bryant and Lynette Bradley's *Children's Reading Problems* is a helpful example.[65] The present book is intended to be another.

## *We need to keep in mind the quality of the text*

There have been valuable advances in understanding the different ways in which texts 'work' for children and these advances also need to be retained and built upon. Many influential theories about children's books come from literary studies, but Katharine Perera's recent work shows what linguistic studies can offer to the understanding of rhythm, words, grammar and style in young children's books. Nicholas Tucker[66] has added many insights into how children's books can meet and reflect children's psychological development. Writers like John Rowe Townsend and Humphrey Carpenter[67] have provided distinctive historical perspectives on children's literature. Too often, these points of view are treated separately in education; together they can create an invaluable professional synthesis for helping to understand the links between reader and text, within the broader triangle of written communication. The recent interest in rhyme and alliteration gives a timely opportunity for psychology, linguistics and literary studies to be exploited in examining the significance of rhyme in children's language and literacy development.[68]

## *Someone needs to write about the writing system*

Finally, the increased influence of psychology in literacy studies might also be promoted from a greater use of linguistic knowledge. There is a tendency in teacher education for many books on literacy to take the writing system for granted. Some teacher education courses on language and literacy do not attend to the English writing system at all. I referred earlier to the NFER report[69] which, like its successor, *What Teachers in Training Are Taught*

*About Reading,*[70] implies criticism of initial teacher training booklists for not including anything which deals in any detail with the relationships between the sound system (the phonology) and the spelling system (the orthography). Yet a wider search suggests that no such book exists in a suitable format. As a consequence, books like Frank Smith's *Reading*, with its chapter on the 'fallacy of phonics', may engender a sense of despair which is in some ways unsound, if the pun may be forgiven.

English spelling is far more patterned than many people seem to assume, especially when account is taken of units of meaning and groups of adjacent letters. Teachers will benefit from more than their own, 'intuitive' knowledge in helping children to tackle reading and writing. We need to avoid further instances of simplistic sloganizing – about 'real books' or phonics or whatever. Instead, we need a scholarly and readable book on the English spelling system, to fill a gap and to bring a sense of proportion to professional understanding of how the system works.[71] We need a realistic recognition that English spelling is patterned in subtle ways, with several systems being drawn upon, and that learning to read and write may not be as easy, nor as 'natural', as some writers have suggested. This framework of accessible knowledge would help to show what the contribution of other disciplines can be – and would provide an informative basis for establishing psychology's role in assisting children to learn the literacy on which so much depends.

NOTES

1   Gorman, T. 1989: *What Teachers in Training Read About Reading* (Occasional Paper No. 4), Slough: National Foundation for Educational Research.
2   Brooks, G., Gorman, T., Kendall, L. and Tate, A. 1992: *What Teachers in Training are Taught About Reading*, Slough: National Foundation for Educational Research.
3   Waterland, L. 1988: *Read With Me: An Apprenticeship Approach to Reading*, 2nd edn, Stroud: Thimble Press.
4   E.g. Beard, R. 1990: *Developing Reading 3–13*, 2nd edn, Sevenoaks: Hodder and Stoughton; Beard, R. (ed.) 1993: *Teaching Literacy: Balancing Perspecitves*, Sevenoaks: Hodder and Stoughton.

5  E.g. Hynds, J. 1988: 'In pursuit of a little understanding', *Books for Keeps*, 52, 4–5.

6  Department of Education and Science 1990: *English in the National Curriculum*, London: Her Majesty's Stationary Office, p. 28.

7  See note 4.

8  Tizard, B., Blatchford, P., Burke, J., Farquhar, C. and Plewis, I. 1988: *Young Children at School in the Inner City*, London: Lawrence Erlbaum Associates.

9  Department of Education and Science 1991: *The Teaching and Learning of Reading in Primary Schools: A Report by Her Majesty's Inspectors*, London: Department of Education and Science.

10  See note 8, p. 169.

11  See note 9, p. 7.

12  Perera, K. 1993: 'The "good book": linguistic aspects', in R. Beard (ed.), *Teaching Literacy: Balancing Perspecitves*, Sevenoaks: Hodder and Stoughton.

13  Meek, M. 1982: *Learning to Read*, London: Bodley Head.

14  Meek, M. 1988: *How Texts Teach What Readers Learn*, Stroud: Thimble Press.

15  Meek, M., Armstrong, S., Ansterfield, V., Graham, J. and Plackett, E. 1983: *Achieving Literacy*, London: Routledge and Kegan Paul.

16  Clay, M.M. 1966: cited in W. Teale and E. Sulzby 1986: *Emergent Literacy: Writing and Reading*, Norwood, NJ: Lawrence Erlbaum Associates.

17  Heath, S.B. 1983: *Ways With Words*, Cambridge: Cambridge University Press.

18  Clay, M.M. 1972: *Reading: The Patterning of Complex Behaviour*, London: Heinemann Educational; Clay, M.M. 1975: *What Did I Write? Beginning Writing Behaviour*, Auckland, New Zealand: Heinemann Educational; Clay, M.M. 1979: *The Early Detection of Reading Difficulties: A Diagnostic Survey with Recovery Procedures*, 2nd edn, Auckland, New Zealand: Heinemann.

19  Stenhouse, L. 1975: *An Introduction to Curriculum Research and Development*, London: Heinemann, p. 116.

20  Hammersley, M. 1992: *What's Wrong With Ethnography?*, London: Routledge.

21  See note 4.

22  E.g. Goodman, K.S. 1967: 'Reading: a psycholinguistic guessing game', *Journal of the Reading Specialist*, 4, 126–35; Goodman, K. 1986: *What's Whole in Whole Language?*, Ontario: Scholastic Publications.

23  Smith, F. 1971: Understanding Reading, New York: Holt, Rinehart and Winston (4th edn, 1988); Smith, F. (ed.) 1973: *Psycholinguistics and Reading*, New York: Holt, Rinehart and Winston; Smith, F. 1978: *Reading*, Cambridge: Cambridge University Press; Smith, F. 1982: *Writing and the Writer*, London: Heinemann.

24  E.g. Skinner, B.F. 1953: *Science and Human Behaviour*, New York: Macmillan.

25  E.g. Bloomfield, L. 1933: *Language*, New York: Holt, Rinehart and Winston.

26  Chomsky, A.N. 1957: *Syntactic Structures*, The Hague: Mouton. See also Chomsky's celebrated 1959 review of Skinner's *Verbal Behaviour* in *Language*, 35, 26–58.

27  Adams, M.J. 1991: 'Why not phonics *and* whole language?', in W. Ellis (ed.), *All Language and the Creation and Literacy*, Baltimore, MD: Orton Dyslexia Society.

28  Ibid.

29  Gibson, E.J. and Levin, H. 1975: *The Psychology of Reading*, Cambridge, MA: MIT Press.

30  Gough, P. 1981: 'A comment on Kenneth Goodman', in M.L. Kamil (ed.), *Directions in Reading: Research and Instruction*, Washington, DC: National Reading Conference, 92–5.

31  Reid, J. 1993: 'Reading and spoken language: the nature of the links', in R. Beard (ed.), *Teaching Literacy: Balancing Perspectives*, Sevenoaks: Hodder and Stoughton.

32  Morris, J.M. 1979: 'New phonics for old', in D.V. Thackray (ed.), *Growth in Reading*, London: Ward Lock Educational.

33  Perera, K. 1980: 'Review of Smith, F. (1978) *Reading*', *Journal of Linguistics*, 16, 127–31.

34  Stott, D.H. 1981: 'Teaching reading: the psycholinguistic invasion', *Reading*, 15 (3), 19–25.

35  Ehri, L. 1991: in L. Rieben and C.A. Perfetti (eds), *Learning to Read: Basic Research and Its Implications*, Hillsdale, NJ: Lawrence Erlbaum Associates, 61–2.

36  Stanovich, K. 1980: 'Towards an interactive-compensatory model of individual differences in the development of reading fluency', *Reading Research Quarterly*, 19, 32–71.

37  Oakhill, J.V. and Garnham, A. 1988: *Becoming a Skilled Reader*, Oxford: Basil Blackwell; see also Yuill, N.M. and Oakhill, J.V. 1991: *Children's Problems in Text Comprehension: An Experimental Investigation*, Cambridge: Cambridge University Press.

38  Goodman, K. 1993: *Phonics Phacts*, Ontario: Scholastic Publications.

39  See note 27.

40  See note 3.

41  Makins, V. 1988: 'New readers start here', *Times Educational Supplement*, 8 April, p. 19.

42  National Curriculum Council 1989: *English Key Stage 1: Non-Statutory Guidance*, York: National Curriculum Council.

43  Personal communication.

44  See note 1.

45  Beard, R. and Oakhill, J. 1994: *Reading by Apprenticeship? A Critique of the 'Apprenticeship Approach' to the Teaching of Reading*. Slough: National Foundation for Educational Research.

46  See note 1, p. 7.

47  See note 12.

48  See note 3, p. 43.

49  Vygotsky, L.S. 1978: *Mind in Society*, translated by Cole, M. et al, Cambridge, MA: Harvard University Press.

50  Edwards, D. and Mercer, N. 1987: *Common Knowledge*, London: Methuen.

51 Vygotsky, L.S. 1962: *Thought and Language*, Cambridge, MA: MIT Press, 180–1.

52 E.g. Mattingly, I.G. 1972: 'Reading, the linguistic process and linguistic awareness', in J.F. Kavanagh and I.G. Mattingly (eds), *Language by Ear and by Eye*, Cambridge, MA: MIT Press; Downing, J. and Valtin, R. (eds) 1984: *Language Awareness and Learning to Read*, New York: Springer.

53 See note 3.

54 E.g. Chall, J.S. 1967: *Learning to Read: The Great Debate*, New York: McGraw-Hill (2nd edn, 1983); Chall, J.S. 1979: 'The great debate: ten years later, with a modest proposal for reading stages', in L.B. Resnick and P.A. Weaver (eds), *Theory and Practice in Early Reading*, vol.1, Hillsdale, NJ: Lawrence Erlbaum Associates; Carbo, M. 1988: 'Debunking the great phonics myth', *Phi Delta Kappan*, 70, 226–40; Chall, J.S. 1989: 'Learning to read: the great debate twenty years later. A response to "Debunking the great phonics myth"', *Phi Delta Kappan*, 71, 521–38; Adams, M.J. 1990: *Beginning to Read: Thinking and Learning About Print*, Cambridge, MA: MIT Press; see also note 9.

55 See note 3, p. 35.

56 Berdiansky, B., Cronnel, B. and Koehler, J. 1969: 'Spelling–sound relations and primary form-class descriptions for speech-comprehension vocabularies of 6–9 year olds', South West Regional Laboratory for Educational Research and Development, Technical Report 15, cited in F. Smith 1971: *Understanding Reading*, New York: Holt, Rinehart and Winston.

57 Albrow, K.H. 1972: *The English Writing System: Notes Towards a Description*, London: Longman, for the Schools Council.

58 Goswami, U. and Bryant, P.E. 1990: *Phonological Skills and Learning to Read*, Hove: Lawrence Erlbaum Associates.

59 See note 54.

60 See note 9.

61 See note 54.

62 Temple, C.A. 1993: *The Beginnings of Writing*, 3rd edn, Needham Heights, MA: Allyn and Bacon, esp. ch. 4.

63 See for instance the *Journal of Research in Reading*, 16 (2), September 1993.

64 Stahl, S.A., Osborn, J. and Lehr, F. 1990: *Beginning to Read: Thinking and Learning About Print – A Summary*, Urbana-Champaign, IL: University of Illinois Center for the Study of Reading.

65 Bryant, P.E. and Bradley, L. 1985: *Children's Reading Problems*, Oxford: Basil Blackwell.

66 Tucker, N. 1981: *The Child and the Book*, Cambridge: Cambridge University Press.

67 Townsend, J.R. 1989: *Written for Children*, London: Bodley Head. Carpenter, H. 1985: *Secret Gardens*, Oxford: Oxford University Press.

68 E.g. Beard, R. (ed.) 1995: *Rhyme, Reading and Writing*, London: Hodder and Stoughton.

69 See note 1.

70 See note 2.

71  Detailed analyses are available (e.g. Albrow, K. 1972: *The English Writing System: Notes Towards a Description*, London: Longman, for the Schools Council; Venezky, R. 1970: *The Structure of English Orthography*, The Hague: Mouton), but there is no source which thoroughly applies this kind of analysis to educational contexts and issues like the teaching of phonics and invented spelling. One of the most significant starts to such an application has been made by Joyce Morris in *The Morris-Montessori Word List* (London: Montessori Centre, 1990). Some published teaching approaches provide some introductory details (e.g. Mackay, D., Thompson, B. and Schaub, P. 1979: *Breakthrough to Literacy: Teacher's Manual*, 2nd edn, London: Longman, for the Schools Council), but these normally only set out lists of phonemes, perhaps with some letter groups which are commonly associated with them.

# 2

## Recognizing Printed Words Unlocks the Door to Reading: How Do Children Find the Key?

Morag Stuart

*Traditionally,* developmental *psychologists have been interested to learn how reading is acquired and what abilities a child needs in order to learn to read. In contrast,* cognitive *psychologists have been most concerned to understand the processes involved in skilled reading: in particular, how a skilled reader recognizes familiar written words, and how new words are learned. In this chapter, Morag Stuart combines the traditional approaches of cognitive and developmental psychology by asking what a child needs to learn in order to develop the skilled reading processes revealed in cognitive psychology.*

*First she reviews the work of developmental psychology on the study of phonological awareness (the ability to manipulate the sounds of the language), letter-sound knowledge, and the role of this knowledge in learning to read. Although reading might appear to be predominantly a visual task, it has been shown that an ability to manipulate the sounds of spoken language forms an essential part of learning to read, and that a failure to develop such awareness can seriously delay reading development.*

*She then discusses the influence of cognitive psychology on the study of lexical (or whole word) and sublexical (or part-word) reading processes available to the skilled reader. This approach takes the view that skilled readers develop a lexicon, or word store, of familiar written word forms that allows words to be recognized, understood and named aloud. Novel written words (which, by virtue of their novelty, are not represented in the lexicon) have to be learned and remembered, and are pronounced initially by using knowledge about how letters and letter groups are typically pronounced. This sub-word knowledge is referred to as sublexical knowledge.*

*Morag Stuart then asks two questions: (1) How do methods of teaching reading affect the child's ability to develop the lexical and sublexical processes available to the skilled reader? (2) How do these processes develop in the child, and how can their development be assessed so that ultimately successful reading can be assured? In answering these questions, the issues are brought vividly to life through the mistakes children make in the process of learning to read.*

*The reader should be aware that, in chapter 3, Philip Seymour and Henryka Evans adopt a rather different view of processes in skilled reading. However, in principle they agree with the view put forward in this chapter that children learning to read need to develop both lexical and sublexical processes.*

I met Martha in 1983 when she was 4½ years old and I went to collect data in her nursery class. This was at the beginning of a longitudinal research project[1] looking at the early development of reading. I wanted to see which 4 year olds were able to detect rhyme: for example, to tell me that 'jar', 'car' and 'star' rhymed, but 'tree', 'boat' and 'sock' didn't. I wanted to see whether if I showed them a picture (e.g. of a dog) they could give me a rhyme for it (log, pog). I wanted to see whether they could tell me the first sound of a set of spoken words that all began with the same sound, for example, tell me that 'wire', 'wheel' and 'watch' all begin with 'w'.

Martha was one of the children who could do all these things with ease. Not all of the 4 year olds could: one in three of the children I tested was unable to detect and produce rhymes; three out of four were unable to tell me the first sounds of words. This no doubt fails to surprise you! But what has it got to do with reading?

What I was testing in the nursery was the children's 'phonological awareness'. Being 'phonologically aware' implies an ability to decentre from the meanings of spoken words, and instead to reflect on and analyse their sound patterns. So, the phonologically aware child knows the meaning of 'cat' – a furry domestic animal that miaows and purrs – and also knows that the spoken word 'cat' rhymes with 'lat', 'pat' and 'tat', and begins with the sound 'k'. A child who is not phonologically aware is conscious only of the meaning of 'cat', and cannot consciously relate the form of the spoken word to other similar spoken forms.

## Phonological Awareness and Reading Development

Since the early 1970s, psychologists have been interested in the relationship between phonological awareness and reading ability. The earliest published studies all demonstrated that, for any age of schoolchild, good readers were better at manipulating the sounds in spoken words than poor readers. For the youngest children, this showed up as better performance in rhyme detection and production tasks; for the oldest children, it showed up as better performance on much more difficult tasks such as omitting sounds in certain positions from the pronunciation of a given target word – for example, omitting 'n' from 'went', 's' from 'cast'. Another example of a more difficult task that differentiates between older good and poor readers is that of reversing the sequence of sounds in a word – repeating 'tip' as 'pit', or 'pain' as 'naip'.

These early correlational studies were not designed to examine cause and effect. All we know from such studies is that the two things, phonological awareness and reading ability, are associated with each other. They tend to go together. Being good at one means you will probably be good at the other. But we cannot tell from this whether it is being good at reading that makes you good at phonological awareness tasks, or whether it is being good at phonological awareness tasks that makes you good at reading.

### Bradley and Bryant's study of phonological awareness and learning to read

However, in 1983, Lynette Bradley and Peter Bryant from Oxford published the results of a longitudinal study[2] which established a causal connection between phonological awareness and success in learning to read and spell. They showed that if you improved children's phonological awareness, their reading also improved. First they identified a large group of 4 and 5 year olds who were completely unable to detect rhyme or alliteration. They put these children into four groups, and trained them over a period of two years.

The training for one group sought to make children more aware of sound segments in spoken words. The children in this group were taught to recognize that for example 'cat', 'hat', 'bat' and 'rat' shared a rhyming segment, and that for example 'bat', 'bee' and 'bone' began with the same 'b' sound.

In the second training group, these sound categorization tasks were accompanied by plastic letters, so that children were also taught that when a sound changed in a spoken word, so a letter changed in the written word. The connection between sound analysis and reading was made quite explicit for this group.

The third training group was a control group, in which children were taught to classify pictures into semantic categories: for example, to group together 'farm animals'. This control condition was included since, if it is phonological awareness that leads to improved success in learning to read, then training children in semantic categorization should not make any difference to their progress in reading.

The fourth group was another control group in which no intervention was made.

Bradley and Bryant were able to show that the children in group one, whose training aimed to develop just their awareness of sounds in spoken words, were somewhat better readers and spellers two years later than children in the two control groups. But the most dramatic gains were made by group two children, whose training included making links between changes of sound and changes of letter. This work is presented in more detail and most accessibly in Bryant and Bradley's 1985 book, *Children's Reading Problems*.[3] Suffice it to say here that, for the first time, Bradley and Bryant had demonstrated convincingly that improving children's ability to manipulate sound segments of spoken words, and to link sound segments with letters, caused them to become better readers and spellers.

Their results have now been replicated by several training studies in several different countries: in Sweden, by Lundberg and
colleagues;[4] in Australia, by Byrne and colleagues;[5,6] and in
America, by Ball and Blachman[7] and Cunningham.[8]

The link between phonological awareness and success in learning to read is robust. It remains strong when differences in IQ
between children are allowed for;[9] it cannot be accounted for by
social class differences,[10] nor by differences in general language
ability.[11]

Given this, you will not be surprised to learn that Martha, an
ordinary north London child, took to reading like a duck to water,
devouring forty-five reading books in her first six months at
school, and achieving a reading age of $6\frac{1}{2}$ years after just nine
months in school.


## Letter-sound Knowledge and Reading Development


But Martha in the nursery had not just been adept at analysing
spoken words. She also knew quite a lot about the way that speech
sounds mapped onto letters. In informal games we played she
was able to write the letters for some sounds I dictated. Mapping
speech sounds onto letters, remember, was the bit of teaching
that had made most difference to subsequent reading and spelling
in the Bradley and Bryant training study. And, by the end of her
first term at school, when I showed Martha letters written on
cards and asked her to tell me the sound that went with each
letter, she already knew the sounds for twenty-three of the twenty-
six letters of the alphabet. So, does phonological awareness matter after all? Or is knowledge of letter sounds the only important
influence? This is a difficult question to answer, because most 4
and 5 year olds who are phonologically aware are like Martha:
they also know quite a lot about letter sounds. However, Bryan
Byrne and Ruth Fielding-Barnsley's training study[12] looked at the
separate contributions of phonological awareness and letter-sound
knowledge to improvements in reading.

## Byrne and Fielding-Barnsley's studies of phonological awareness and letter-sound knowledge

Byrne and Fielding-Barnsley trained 4-year-old pre-school children to notice alliteration (e.g. that 'sun' and 'sail' start with the same sound) and its equivalent at the ends of words (e.g. that 'drum' and 'broom' end with the same sound). The training programme lasted for only twelve weeks, with one session per week. The children were trained in groups of four to six. They were taught to recognize six sounds, 's', 'm', 't', 'l', 'p' and 'a', at the beginning and end of words. They were also taught to associate these six sounds with the letters that represent them, S, M, T, L, P and A.

At the end of the training period, the children were given three tests. The first assessed their ability to report sounds occurring at the beginning and end of spoken words. The second assessed their knowledge of the six letter sounds they had been taught. The third assessed their ability to use their sound analysis ability and letter-sound knowledge in a reading task. They were shown pairs of written words beginning with one of the six letters they had been taught, for example 'sow' and 'mow', and asked to point to the word that said 'mow'.

Generally speaking, children were only successful on this third task if they had passed *both* the sound task *and* the sound-to-letter matching task.

In a later follow-up study[13] the trained children were significantly better readers and spellers at the end of the school year than those untrained children who still failed the sound analysis test despite a year's tuition in reading.

By using regression analysis (a statistical technique in which the separate contribution of several different variables can be assessed) Byrne and Fielding-Barnsley were able to show that, once the variance in reading and spelling scores that was due to IQ or to sound-to-letter mapping knowledge had been taken out of the equation, there was still a significant effect of sound analysis.

They conclude from this that phonological awareness plays a separate role in reading and spelling development, and is important in its own right, even though knowledge of the relations between sounds and letters is also important. Both things are necessary for children to become good readers and spellers.

The other important thing to emphasize from the work of Byrne and Fielding-Barnsley is that although they only used six sounds in their training programme, children who successfully passed the sound analysis task at the end of this training could categorize words that began or ended with other sounds. That is, they had learnt a principle which they could apply in all cases.

### Summary so far

There is now a substantial body of work that demonstrates a causal connection between young children's phonological awareness and ability to map sounds onto letters, and their success in learning to read. This chain of causality is well established; but how does it operate? Why do the first two things (phonological awareness, sound-to-letter mapping knowledge) lead to the third (success in learning to read)? At present, we have more than one possible answer to this question! All suggest that the causal connection has to do with the fact that phonological awareness and understanding how sounds map onto letters equip children to take advantage of the alphabetic system.

### Alphabets

Alphabets have evolved as writing systems precisely to exploit possible relations between the units of spoken and written language. This can be done at different levels: for example in Japanese there are two written symbol systems for representing spoken syllables. However, most modern written languages attempt to capture the relations between single speech sounds (phonemes) and the written symbols that represent them (graphemes). This can be done with more or less consistency. If you are fortunate enough to be born into an Italian-speaking family, then the phonemes in your language will map onto graphemes in an entirely consistent way. If you are unlucky enough to be born into an English-speaking family, then you have to learn to cope with an inconsistent alphabetic system: with 'break' and 'freak', with 'laugh', 'knife' and 'doubt'.


## Larger Phonological Segments: Onsets and Rimes


It has frequently been suggested that there is more consistency in English if we look at spoken segments larger than the phoneme, and the spelling patterns that correspond to these larger segments. The spoken segments that have received particular attention in recent years are the sub-syllabic units of onset and rime.

Linguists tell us that spoken syllables are not just linear sequences of phonemes but have a hierarchical organization. For example, 'cap' is not just a three-phoneme sequence k-a-p, and 'string' is not just a five-phoneme sequence s-t-r-i-ng. There is another structural level between these single phonemes and the level of the syllable. This intermediate level consists of the two elements of onset and rime. The onset is the opening consonant or consonants of a syllable. So, the onset of 'cap' is 'k', which coincides with a single phoneme. The onset of 'string' is 'str' which contains three phonemes. The rime is the vowel and any following consonants. So, the rime of 'cap' is 'ap' and the rime of 'string' is 'ing'.

Rebecca Treiman in America has shown in a series of carefully controlled experimental studies[14] that young children are sensitive to onsets and rimes. You can demonstrate this quite easily yourself by asking 4 year olds to tell you the beginning sound of words like 'skate' or 'plum': many 4 year olds will tell you that 'skate' begins with 'sk' and 'plum' with 'pl'. It is quite difficult for pre-readers to split complex onsets like this into the single phonemes that make them up.

And, of course, the ability to detect and produce rhyme depends on being sensitive to the second sub-syllabic unit, the rime. 'Cap' rhymes with 'tap' and 'string' with 'thing' precisely because the two share the same rime.

## Rhyme and Reading

Usha Goswami suggests that once children can put words into rhyming categories, they will expect words which share the same spelling pattern (which look alike) to rhyme (to sound alike). She has demonstrated this in several experiments with infant school children.[15] Typically, she shows the children a 'clue' word, for example 'beak', which she pronounces for them. The children are told this 'clue' word will help them to read the other words they are shown.

She then asks them to read three kinds of word. One set contains words which rhyme with 'beak' and are also spelt with '-eak': words like 'peak' and 'weak'. One set contains words which have the same first three letters as 'beak', pronounced in the same way: words like 'bean' and 'bead'. The last set is of words which also share three letters with 'beak' but scramble the order, so that the pronunciation changes: words like 'lake' and 'bask'.

The 5 year olds she tested were all pre-readers, unable to read any words on a standardized reading test. Nevertheless, they were sometimes able to read the words that rhymed with the clue word. That is, they could make analogies. If the end of a word looked the same as the end of the clue word, they expected it to rhyme with the clue word.

The 6 and 7 year olds were able to make analogies also where the beginning three letters were shared. They were better at reading words like 'bean' and 'bead', given 'beak' as a clue, than words like 'lake' and 'bask'. And they still showed an extra advantage for words that rhymed with the clue word, that shared the linguistic unit of rime with the clue word.

Reading new words that have never been seen before by analogy with words already known is a powerful strategy, but on its own it is not sufficient to ensure that a new word will be correctly pronounced. 'Weak' and 'break' look alike, but they do not rhyme; nor do 'bough' 'tough' 'cough' 'through' and 'though'. Even at the level of spelling patterns for onsets and rimes, English does not provide consistent relationships between spelling and sound. So, how do children learn to read English words, when the same spelling pattern is pronounced differently in different words?

## Two Ways to Recognize Printed Words

One model of the reading process which allows us to think clearly about this is the dual-route model, first set out by John Morton[16] and much refined and elaborated since then. The dual-route model is not a model of the processes involved in learning to read: it is a model of the fully fledged reading system of the skilled adult reader. As such, it is useful to those of us who are interested in how children learn to read in that it gives us a tried and tested model of the processes and structures that the child must create in order to become a reader. However, we will need to look beyond this model in order to begin to understand how these processes and structures are created.

In the dual-route model, there are, paradoxically, three ways in which printed words can be recognized. It is called a dual-route model because two of these three ways involve dealing with whole words, and they are therefore grouped together as 'lexical' (i.e. 'whole word') routes. The subdivision of lexical routes into two ways of recognizing printed words is relevant if we are talking about the damaged reading systems of adult patients, some of whom can read irregularly spelt words aloud correctly without understanding their meaning. However, this degree of complexity is not essential to understanding the arguments put forward in this chapter. The two lexical routes will therefore be treated as a single system for processing whole words.

## Lexical Word Recognition

We can recognize many words simply because we have read them so often before that we know them. A useful way of thinking about this is to say that we have created 'logogens' for them. A logogen is a device dedicated to collecting evidence that a particular printed word is present. For example, suppose that you have repeatedly come across the word 'fish' in your reading. Now, whenever you see the word 'fish', the logogen you have created

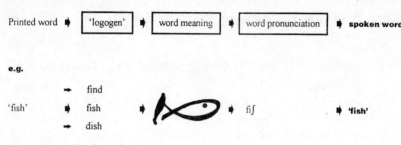

*Figure 2.1* The lexical route

to recognize it gets excited, because every part of the printed word 'fish' corresponds to every part of the evidence that the logogen is set to collect. Although the logogens that you have created for similarly spelt words like 'find' and 'dish' will be excited to some extent, the logogen for 'fish' will reach its preset criterion first, because every bit of the stimulus presented matches its requirements. So the logogen for 'fish' will 'fire'.[17] This means it will send a message on to the semantic system, where word meanings are stored, and allow you to retrieve the meaning of 'fish'. Retrieving the meaning sends a message on to the store of word pronunciations, and this allows you to pronounce the word correctly (figure 2.1).

Dual-route theorists call this way of recognizing words the lexical route. It processes words as wholes, and it allows us to retrieve meaning directly from seeing a printed word. Whole printed words are recognized as such by their logogens; meanings of whole words are stored in and retrieved from the semantic system; pronunciations of whole words are stored in and retrieved from the pronunciation store.

This route capitalizes on our knowledge of spoken language. We have already stored meanings and pronunciations of words, because we can understand and produce speech. What we need to create in order to become readers as well as speakers of our language is a system for recognizing printed words, and processes that allow this system to access our ready stored knowledge of meanings and pronunciations. In dual-route terminology, we need to create logogens and ways for logogens to access meaning and pronunciation.

## Sublexical Word Recognition

But we must have a second way of recognizing printed words, because we can read aloud words that we have never seen in print before. At the extreme, we can read aloud strings of letters that a psychologist has invented in order to assess our ability to pronounce novel letter strings: things like 'smon', 'gupont', 'wipasult' and 'chaiversikight'. We cannot be reading either words we have never seen before or invented letter strings by the lexical route. Why not? Because this lexical route can only operate if we have formed a logogen, a recognition device, for the word we are looking at. We cannot have formed a logogen for a word we have never seen before, or for an invented letter string, because logogens are formed from repeated exposure to printed words. When we have seen a word often enough to commit its printed form to memory, the logogen IS this memory. Therefore, if we have never seen a word before, we cannot possibly have a logogen to recognize it, to 'fire', and send a message to the semantic system to retrieve the meaning for us.

The solution to this problem, according to dual-route theory, is to suggest that we do indeed have a second way of processing written stimuli. We can parse letter strings into printed segments that map onto spoken segments, and we can blend the spoken segments together to produce a pronunciation. There are three important elements to this procedure: (1) parsing the letter string into the correct segments; (2) mapping these segments of print onto the sounds they represent; and (3) blending the sounds into a whole pronunciation. We know rather little about how the letter string parsing mechanism works, except that it must be a complex mechanism. Sometimes the segments of print that we need to map onto sound are single letters. This is the case with the first three of my invented letter strings, 'smon', 'gupont' and 'wipasult'. Sometimes we need to take two, three or four letters together in order to map onto a single phoneme. This is the case with all words where there are more letters than phonemes: words like 'church', which has six letters but only three phonemes (ch ur ch); words like 'fight', which has five letters but again only three phonemes (f igh t); or words like 'eight' which has five letters but only two phonemes (eigh t). The letters that need to be taken together to map onto a single phoneme in words such as these are called 'graphemes'. So, 'church' has six letters but three graphemes (*ch ur ch*); and so on.

The fact that you can correctly pronounce my fourth invented letter string 'chaiversikight' is evidence that skilled readers can parse letter strings into graphemes that map onto phonemes. If you were unable to do this, you would have to take each letter separately and attempt to assemble a pronunciation for 'chaiversikight' from k-h-a-i-v-e-r-s-i-g-h-t. What remains unknown is how the ability to parse written words into their correct segments for translation to sound develops normally in children.

By pronouncing my novel letter strings correctly, you have also demonstrated that you have some system for finding phonemes that correspond to graphemes, for mapping between print and sound below the level of the whole word. And you have demonstrated your ability to blend phonemes together and achieve a complete pronunciation. We have some ideas about how these processes might be developed normally in children. One candidate is that teachers sometimes teach children 'phonics', correspondences between print and sound below the level of the whole word. Sometimes, phonic teaching includes practice in blending phonemes together to achieve a pronunciation. However, it is also possible that at least some children may be able to infer grapheme–phoneme correspondences from their own experience of printed words, without needing explicit teaching. This is an idea that Jackie Masterson, Philip Quinlan and I are currently investigating.

These processes of phonological recoding from print to sound take place in what dual-route theorists call the sublexical (i.e. dealing with sub-word units) route (figure 2.2). This route does not allow us to go directly to the meaning of a word: we must pronounce the word before we can retrieve its meaning. Nor does it deal in whole words until a pronunciation has been achieved: it deals in segments of printed words and relates these to segments of sound.

This route is also intimately linked with our spoken language system. The pronunciations we assemble feed into our system for understanding and producing speech. Normally, this will access the correct meaning of the word we intend to read. However,

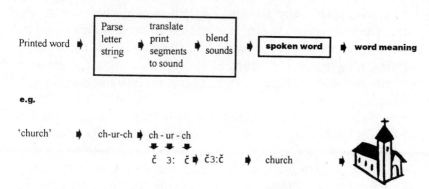

*Figure 2.2* The sublexical route

words which do not obey the rules for translating from print to sound will be mispronounced when read by the sublexical route, even if the system itself is working perfectly. Examples would be words like 'cough' or 'gauge'. Sometimes our mispronunciations will resemble a real word. We might, for example, recode the word 'gauge' as 'gorge', since 'au' usually says 'or'. If we do this, then we will access the meaning of 'gorge' not 'gauge'. We will think of a deep and narrow valley, not a measuring instrument. However, because both lexical and sublexical routes operate together, in tandem, this will normally result only in a delay while we resolve the conflict between the correct meaning ('measuring instrument') accessed by the lexical route and the incorrect meaning ('deep and narrow valley') accessed by the sublexical route.

## Why We Need Two Ways of Recognizing Printed Words

Why do we need two routes, two qualitatively different ways of recognizing, understanding and pronouncing written words? Dual-route theorists argue that we need a lexical route because, at least if we are reading in English, the nature of the language seems to require it. In English there are many inconsistent and irregular words, which do not obey rules of spelling-to-sound correspondence at any level except that of the whole word. We can only pronounce 'though' correctly if we have learned it off by heart, which, according to dual-route theory, means that we have created a logogen for it which has a well-specified representation of 'though' which allows us to retrieve its meaning and then its pronunciation.

Dual-route theorists argue that we need a sublexical route because this is the only way to read new words that we have never seen in print before: try 'sutler', 'swaraj', 'trichiasis' and 'knag'. . . . You may not be sure you've said them correctly, but you couldn't have begun to find them in your logogen system, which cannot have formed a representation for words never yet encountered in print. And, although by sublexical processing you can make a shot at pronouncing these new words, you would have to look them up in the dictionary if you wanted to know their meanings. As in the case of the mistakes cited above, you get to the meaning after the pronunciation.

## Evidence that Skilled Readers Do Have Two Ways of Recognizing Printed Words

There is evidence from experiments with skilled readers that both routes exist. This has been investigated by comparing the performance of skilled adults on reading aloud regular words, irregular words and nonwords. Regular words are words whose pronunciation is predictable from their spelling (e.g. 'bead', 'lemon', 'janitor' and 'peripatetic'). Irregular words are words whose correct pronunciation cannot be arrived at by use of spelling-to-sound rules (e.g. 'two', 'answer', 'colonel' and 'pneumonia'). Nonwords are pronounceable letter strings that psychologists make up (e.g. 'smon', 'gupont', 'wipasult' and 'chaiversikight') (figure 2.3).

Typically, skilled adult readers read regular words more quickly than irregular words or nonwords. One explanation of this finding is that irregular words can only be correctly read by the lexical route, which deals in whole words. Any attempt to read them by translating from spelling segments to sound segments will result

| Irregular words | Regular words | Nonwords |
|---|---|---|
| e.g. **pint**<br>**borough**<br>**come**<br>**have** | e.g. **went**<br>**lemon**<br>**shampoo**<br>**house** | e.g. **swun**<br>**keppot**<br>**leeb**<br>**draize** |

*Figure 2.3* Horses for courses

in an incorrect pronunciation (for example t*W*o, ans*W*er, col-on-el, *P*neumonia). Nonwords can only be read at all by translating from spelling segments to sound segments, because they have no representation in the logogen system. Regular words, on the other hand, can be correctly pronounced when read by the lexical route, and when translated from spelling segments to sound segments in the sublexical route. Hence their advantage over the other two types (irregular words and nonwords), which must rely on one or other route only for a correct reading.

The fact that regular words do show an advantage is evidence that written words are always automatically and unconsciously processed by both routes. Sometimes the lexical route will give a faster response, sometimes the sublexical route will. Since regular words can be processed correctly by either route, they will on average be read more quickly.[18]

## Are Lexical and Sublexical Routes the Same as Sight Vocabulary and Phonics?

When we think about inexperienced readers, it is tempting to equate the notion of a sublexical route with the notion of 'phonics',

and the notion of a lexical route with the notion of 'sight vocabulary'. However, there are some important caveats to assuming
that these are indeed identical notions.

There are at least two important differences between 'phonics'
and the concept of a sublexical route. The first and most obvious
difference is that phonics is a method of *teaching* reading. The
sublexical route is not a method of teaching reading, but an established system for assembling the pronunciations of written words,
and so gaining access to their meanings. It may be tempting to
think that the best way of establishing such a system is through
phonic teaching, but this is not necessarily the case, and I know
of no conclusive evidence that it is.

Second, phonic teaching aims to supply the learner with a strategy for working out the pronunciation of previously unseen
written words. The sublexical route is not a strategic option that
the skilled reader can choose to implement or not: it is a fully
automatic processing system which is always triggered by the
stimulus of the printed word, whether this word was previously
known to the reader or not.

The apparent similarities between phonics and the sublexical
route seem to exist only because the two share some of the same
terminology. Beyond this superficial level, they may well represent entirely different processes which have no necessary relation
the one to the other. This is certainly true if when we think of
phonics what we have in mind is the effortful and laborious 'sound-
ing-out aloud' of the child struggling to read. The fast, fully
automated and internalized phonological recoding system of the
good reader corresponds better to the dual-route concept of a
sublexical route.

Similarly, 'sight vocabulary' is not necessarily the same as the
lexical route. Both terms imply the existence of a memory for
whole words. In the lexical route, each memory for a word is a
logogen. Each logogen consists of a complete and fully detailed
representation of the word it has been formed to detect. However, observational studies of beginning readers suggest that the
visual memories children form for words in their sight vocabulary are far from complete records of the properties of each word.
For example, in a study of children in their first year at school in

Scotland,[19] who were being taught to read by learning whole words on flashcards and then reading little books that repeated their flashcard vocabulary, Philip Seymour and Leonie Elder showed that children use partial cues to remember whole words. This showed up in the errors they made when presented with single words to read aloud. So, the child who used the two letter L's in 'yellow' as a cue to remember that word also responded 'yellow' when asked to read the word 'ball', and commented 'It's "yellow" because its got two sticks'.

I found similar errors in children in my longitudinal study, the most memorable being a very bright young 5 year old who confidently read 'driver' as 'television'. This was a mistake that several other children had made. However, because Peter was so confident in his response, I asked how he knew it was 'television'. 'Oh,' he replied, 'That's easy. It's got a dot. Actually, television's got two dots, but anyway, I don't care.' Now, if the logogen system that I have developed to recognize words in my lexical route worked on the basis of 'two sticks' or 'a dot' (or maybe two!), I would be hard put to distinguish one word from the next. So, the lexical route certainly does not resemble the beginning reader's early attempts to build a sight vocabulary. At a later stage, when children have formed more detailed representations of printed words, their sight vocabulary will indeed correspond to the dual-route model concept of a lexical route.

## Which Route Develops First?

There seems no good reason to suppose (as certain 'stage' theories of reading development do) that the development of the lexical route must always precede development of the sublexical route, or vice versa. It seems likely that, given certain prerequisites, the two routes can be developed together.

In my longitudinal study, there were children who were able to read nonwords as well as words in their first term at school. These children were obviously developing the two routes in tandem. They were children like Martha, who arrived at school with good phonological awareness and some knowledge of the relationships between single letters and their sounds.

There were also children who relied on the lexical route. If I showed them nonwords, they either responded 'I don't know' or they responded with a visually similar word from their reading vocabulary, reading 'hig' as 'pig' and 'wot' as 'with'. These were children who had arrived at school unaware that spoken words were patterns of sound as well as symbols for meanings, and who tended to know little about the relationships between letters and sounds. In other words, they were not ready to grasp the alphabetic principle when they were first introduced to reading tuition, and so had no option but to rely on the lexical route, dealing only in whole words and direct relations between print and meaning.

## Summary so far

Being phonologically aware and knowing about letter-sound relationships when you first start learning to read carries with it the probability that you will become a good reader. One suggestion as to why this should be so is that we expect words which look alike to sound alike too. So if we know how to read 'cat', we will be able to read 'pat', 'mat' and 'hat' correctly, by analogy with the word 'cat' which we know how to pronounce. However, analogy does not always work: some words that look alike actually sound different: words like 'love' and 'move'; 'come' and 'home'; 'give' and 'dive'. An alternative suggestion is that all skilled readers have two ways of recognizing printed words, which operate automatically and unconsciously in all our interactions with printed text. Children need to develop these two ways of processing print: a lexical route, which accesses meaning directly from the whole letter string; and a sublexical route, which translates from print to sound and accesses meaning once a pronunciation has been achieved.

We now need to consider how phonological awareness and letter–sound knowledge might contribute to the development of these two routes.

# Relation Between Phonological Awareness, Letter-sound Knowledge and the Development of the Lexical Route

## *Stuart and Coltheart's longitudinal study of reading development*

In this longitudinal study,[20] we looked at early development of the lexical route. The database was formed from the mistakes children made when I asked them to read single words which they were familiar with, either because they had met them already several times in their reading books and/or because they had been taught them on flashcards. The mistakes were collected on seven occasions over an eighteen-month period, starting two months after the children began to attend infant school.

We analysed the children's errors into five groups (figure 2.4).

## Group 1 errors: Little visual resemblance to the target word

The first group contained errors that bore little visual resemblance to the word the child had been asked to read. We defined visual resemblance in terms of number and position of shared letters between the word shown to the child and the word given as response. Examples of group 1 errors include those where the presence of a capital letter seemed to signal a name (e.g. reading 'Jane' as 'Justin', or 'Robert' as 'Tommy'); or where the presence of a single letter seemed to have reminded children of their own name or their friend's name (e.g. reading 'a' as 'Christina', or 'hat' as 'John'). They include those where no letters were shared between target and error (e.g. reading 'her' as 'boy', or 'girl' as 'Tommy'); or where just one letter was present in both target and error, but not in the same position in the word (e.g. reading 'milk' as 'lorry', or 'go' as 'on').

One thing that united errors in group 1 was that they were almost invariably other words the child was learning or had been exposed to, as though one of the first things children do is learn which words they are learning to recognize in print.

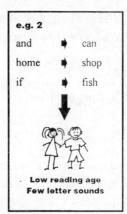

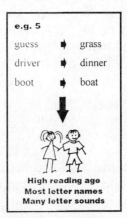

*Figure 2.4* Error groups

Group 1 errors constituted about 20 per cent of the total error collection of some 4000 errors. Some children were more prone than others to make them, and continued making them for far longer into their school careers. These children had the lowest reading ages, and knew little about letter names and letter sounds. Beginning readers need to be able to recognize and name letters in order to pay attention to letters as relevant cues for recognizing printed words. Children who have had little pre-reading exposure to letters are left relying on 'two sticks' for 'yellow', 'a dot' for 'television', a capital letter for a name, or memory of juxtaposition in a reading book for a guess, as in 'milk' for 'lorry'.

## Group 2 errors: One or more letters shared but out of position

The second group (13 per cent of total errors) contained errors that shared more than one letter with the target word shown to the child. Some showed no regard for letter position within the word (e.g. reading 'and' as 'can', 'lollipops' as 'police', 'home' as 'shop', or 'cars' as 'across'). Others showed no regard for letter sequence within the word (e.g. reading 'not' as 'on', 'if' as 'fish', 'liked' as 'milk', or 'yes' as 'see').

Most children made some of these errors in the early months of tuition, but by the end of the first year at school only children with low reading ages and who knew few letter sounds were making many errors like this.

## Group 3 errors: Final letters shared with the target word

The third group (11 per cent of total errors) contained errors where the final letter or letters were shared with the target word. Examples here are reading 'green' as 'open', 'love' as 'have', 'sticky' as 'my', or 'back' as 'look'. Children who persisted in producing errors like this into the second year at school were those whose reading ages were low and who knew fewest letter sounds.

## Group 4 errors: Initial letters shared with the target word

The fourth group (33 per cent of total errors) contained errors where the beginning letter or letters were shared with the target word shown to the child. Examples here include reading 'just' as 'jelly', 'one' as 'on', 'sound' as 'some', 'island' as 'Islington', or 'these' as 'taxi'.

Incidence of group 4 errors did not relate to reading age at all: children with high or low reading ages were equally likely to produce them. However, halfway through the first year at school, those children who knew most letter *names* were also making most group 4 errors. By the beginning of the second year at school, it was the children who knew most letter *sounds* who made most group 4 errors. This may reflect the fact that it is possible to use the first letter either as a visual cue or as a phonological cue. You might remember that 'jelly' begins with the letter J, and then respond 'jelly' to 'just' because 'just' also begins with the letter J. This would explain the relation between letter name knowledge and these errors, which emerged during the first year at school. Or you might sound out the first letter ('just' . . . 'dj') and respond with a word in your spoken vocabulary that begins with 'dj' (jelly). This would explain the relationship between letter-sound knowledge and these errors, which did not emerge until the second year at school.

## Group 5 errors: Initial and final letters shared with the target word

The fifth group (20 per cent of total errors) contained errors where both the initial and final letters were shared with the target word shown to the child. These were the most visually similar to their targets, and included reading 'guess' as 'grass', 'driver' as 'dinner', 'helicopters' as 'hippopotamus', and 'doctor' as 'dinosaur'.

As children's reading developed over the first eighteen months in school, so the proportion of group 5 errors increased. The children with the highest reading ages made mostly group 5 errors. These were also the children who knew most letter names early in the first school year, and who consistently knew most letter sounds, So, the better the child was at reading, the more close visual resemblance there was between the errors made in reading single words aloud and the target words the child had been asked to read. This suggests that the better readers had already begun to develop more detailed representations of the words they were learning to recognize. In the terminology of the dual-route model, they were developing more fully specified logogens.

## 'Good' and 'Bad' Errors

Some errors were indicative of better reading than others. Group 1 errors bore hardly any graphic resemblance to the word shown to the child; group 2 errors showed scant respect for letter position and sequence; and group 3 errors in which final letters were shared could be positively misleading as a source of information.

The child who reads 'love' as 'have' is presumably paying attention to the right-hand side of the written word. Looking at 've' while saying aloud 'have' gives no opportunity of correctly mapping the first spoken sound to the first written letter. Errors in groups 1, 2 and 3 appeared to reflect poor reading ability and were considered to be 'bad' errors.

Errors in groups 4 and 5, which suggested attention was being paid to the first (or first and last) letters appeared to reflect a more promising strategy. Paying attention to the first letter of the written word as the word is spoken might help to associate the first letter of the written word with the first sound of the spoken word. These errors were therefore classified as 'good' errors.

The balance between 'good' and 'bad' errors changed at a certain point in the child's development (figure 2.5). We looked at this by splitting each child's errors on each testing occasion into a set of 'good' errors and a set of 'bad' errors. We looked to see for each child when the balance between these two kinds of error changed: that is, when did the child begin to make more 'good' than 'bad' errors?

This proved to be quite simple, because, by and large, once the balance changed, the child continued to make consistently more 'good' errors on every testing occasion.

The balance changed for each child at the point where children were not only phonologically aware but were also able to tell me the sounds for at least thirteen letters of the alphabet. Martha, for example, who reached this point in the January of her first year in school, made almost exclusively group 4 and 5 errors from then on. She also commented vigorously on what she saw as my misspellings! When I asked her to read 'four', she said, 'You're trying to write "for"! You've added on some more letters. . . . It's a nonsense word.' When I asked her to read 'gun', she read it as 'garden', adding 'you didn't write enough letters'.

So, it looked as though knowing about sounds in spoken words, and knowing about how letters related to those sounds, guided the way children looked at and tried to remember printed words. The specific details recorded in the logogens they formed seemed to depend on their understanding of sound patterns and their knowledge of letter–sound correspondences. Why should this be? How might understanding that spoken words are made up of

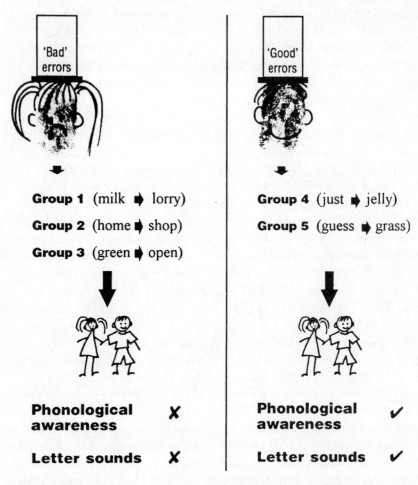

*Figure 2.5* Characteristics of children making 'good' and 'bad' errors

smaller segments of sound which can relate to printed letters help the child to form more detailed and ordered memories of 'whole' printed words?

## Stuart's study of sound-to-letter expectancies

In a later study,[21] I tested the hypothesis that children who do understand this before they have ever been taught to learn to read will expect spoken words to look certain ways when written down. I reasoned that children who knew that 'dog' began with the sound 'd' would expect the written word 'dog' to start with the letter D. Those who knew that 'dog' ended with the sound 'g' would also expect the written word to end with the letter G. This would be true whether or not the child had already seen the written word 'dog'. Just knowing the spoken word, being able to segment some of its sounds, and knowing which letters represented those sounds, would allow a child to 'expect' the written word to contain those letters in certain positions. The child would then be looking to those positions in the written word to confirm their expectancies.

To test this, I worked with 4-year-old pre-readers, none of whom could read any of the words on a standardized reading test. I found children who could tell me that, for example, 'tiger' began with the sound 't', and if you wanted to write 'tiger' you needed to start with the letter T. If I showed them a picture of a pan, and asked them to choose the correct printed word for 'pan' from a choice of 'pan' and 'cut', they could easily do this. They expected 'pan' to start with a letter P. I also found children who could tell me that, for example, the last sound of 'leaf' was 'f', and that if you wanted to write 'leaf' you needed a letter F at the end. If I showed them a picture of a comb, and asked them to choose the correct printed word for 'comb' from a choice of 'cav' (cave) and 'com' (comb), they chose 'com'. They expected 'comb' to end with the letter M. Of course, in standard spelling, it doesn't, it ends with a B! However, it is certainly possible that where your expectancies are dashed, where you anticipate an M and find a B, you will notice and absorb this discrepancy. You will learn irregular spelling patterns precisely because they do not match your regular, sound-based expectancies. In this way, your pre-existing understanding of sound patterns and your knowledge of how sounds relate to letters will affect the development of your lexical route. It does this not only by ensuring that you notice spelling patterns which do not correspond to the sounds you can hear in a word, but by making letter order and sequence salient. Sequential order is intrinsic to understanding and producing spoken words. Awareness of sound patterns seems to impose the necessity for order and sequence upon written words too, and so ensures the creation of fully specified representations in the logogen system that are not misled by anagrams, by 'part' and 'trap', 'who' and 'how', or 'tea', 'eat' and 'ate'.

## Relation Between Phonological Awareness, Letter-sound Knowledge and the Development of the Sublexical Route

These relationships must by now be so obvious as to need little more in the way of comment. Ability to develop a sublexical route depends on the child having some conscious insight into the sound structure of spoken words. It also depends on familiarity with the written symbols, letters, that represent speech sounds. Children without this insight and familiarity will find it more difficult to profit from phonic teaching, as for them this will be learning to match one unknown (the single speech sound) with another (the letter or letters to represent that speech sound). Paradoxically, children *with* this insight and familiarity probably have less need of phonic teaching, as they are more able to infer correspondences between letters and the sounds they represent from their experience of reading text.

## How Can We Assess Whether Children are Successfully Developing these Two Reading Routes?

### Sublexical route development

Two indices of successful development of a sublexical route are (1) good nonword reading and (2) more error-free reading of regularly spelt words compared with irregularly spelt words. Children who are successfully developing a sublexical route should therefore be able to read nonwords, and should show regularity effects when asked to read matched sets of regular and irregular words.

Reading nonwords can be a stressful task for young children, so when I attempted this recently[22] I started with very easy three-letter nonwords, like 'kem'. I had eight lists that gradually got harder, increasing to two syllables rather than one, and introducing consonant clusters such as 'sl' and 'nt' at the beginning or end. Children were allowed to stop whenever they reached a list that they felt was too difficult. I tested twenty-four children aged between 6 and $6\frac{1}{2}$, whose reading ages on a standardized test ranged from 5 years to 11 years 3 months. Twenty of the children were able to read some nonwords correctly, and so were developing sublexical reading routes. The four who were unable to read any nonwords had the lowest reading ages in the group. In fact, there was a strikingly high correlation (0.91) between the children's reading ages and the number of nonwords they could read. This suggests that the better readers among these 6 year olds were the children who had made most progress in sublexical route development.

What about regularity effects? In a recent study of children in their second year at school, from $5\frac{1}{2}$ to $6\frac{1}{2}$ years old, Jackie Masterson, Veronica Laxon and I[23] found that these young readers did indeed show regularity effects when we asked them to read words of medium or low frequency. The children with the highest reading ages showed the largest effects. This again implies that they had better developed sublexical routes.

## Lexical route development

Two indices of successful development of a lexical route are (1) ability to read irregularly spelt words and (2) effects of word frequency on reading. The latter effect depends on the fact that, the more often you access a logogen for a word, the more efficiently the logogen responds. Therefore, words which have been read most frequently in the past will be read more accurately.

The study by Masterson et al. also provided data on lexical route development. All of the children were able to read some irregular words, and must therefore have been developing a lexical reading route. When asked to read high frequency words, children were equally correct on words with regular (e.g. 'horse', 'dance', 'quick') and irregular (e.g. 'laugh', 'come', 'build') spelling patterns. This suggests that for these high frequency words pronunciation was always achieved by the lexical route.

It seems safe to conclude that by the second year of reading instruction, normally developing children will already have in place the information processing systems that skilled readers use. That is, normal 6 year olds are able to use both lexical and sublexical routes to word recognition.

## Five and Six Year Olds We Should Worry About

Studies of the relationship between phonological awareness and reading imply that we should definitely worry about any child who comes into the infant school unable to recognize rhyme. We should worry about children in their first year of the infant school who cannot identify the first sound of a spoken word. We should worry at this stage if children cannot give the name and the sound of single letters of the alphabet.

Studies of early reading development imply that we should worry about children in their first year of school whose errors in single word reading bear little graphic resemblance to the word-to-be-read. We should worry about six year olds who cannot read simple three-letter nonwords.

## . . . and Those We Need Not Worry About

Let us finish on a cheerful note, with Martha, the archetypal child whose reading we need not worry about. As a 10 year old, Martha had a well-established lexical route. She made only one error in reading irregular words of high or medium frequency. She also had a well-established sublexical route, making no errors with low frequency regular words. When reading low frequency irregular words, she sometimes pronounced them as though they were regular, reading 'gauge' as 'gorge', and 'subtle' as 'subtel'. She sometimes read them by analogy with a word she knew, reading 'trough' as 'truf', and 'borough' as 'bruf' (presumably by analogy with 'rough'). She was good at reading nonwords correctly.

I said goodbye to Martha in 1990, when she was 11. Her reading age was $12\frac{1}{2}$, and she read with good comprehension. Early phonological awareness, early knowledge about letters, had set her on a path to success which was maintained right through her primary school career.

NOTES

1   Stuart, M. and Coltheart, M. 1988: 'Does reading develop in a sequence of stages?', *Cognition*, 30, 139–81.
2   Bradley, L. and Bryant, P.E. 1983: 'Categorising sounds and learning to read: a causal connection', *Nature*, 301, 419–21.
3   Bryant, P.E. and Bradley, L. 1985: *Children's Reading Problems*, Oxford: Blackwell.
4   Lundberg, I., Frost, J. and Petersen, O.-P. 1988: 'Effects of an extensive program for stimulating phonological awareness in preschool children', *Reading Research Quarterly*, 23, 263–84.
5   Byrne, B. and Fielding-Barnsley, R. 1991: 'Evaluation of a program to teach phonemic awareness to young children', *Journal of Educational Psychology*, 83, 451–5.
6   Byrne, B. and Fielding-Barnsley, R. 1993: 'Evaluation of a program to teach phonemic awareness to young children: a one-year follow up', *Journal of Educational Psychology*, 85, 104–11.
7   Ball, E.W. and Blachman, B.A. 1991: 'Does phoneme awareness training in kindergarten make a difference in early word recognition and developmental spelling?' *Reading Research Quarterly*, 26, 49–66.
8   Cunningham, A.E. 1990: 'Explicit versus implicit instruction in phonemic awareness', *Journal of Experimental Child Psychology*, 50, 429–44.
9   See note 1.
10  Raz, I.S. and Bryant, P.E. 1990: 'Social background, phonological awareness and children's reading', *British Journal of Developmental Psychology*, 8, 209–25.
11  Bryant, P.E., MacLean, M. and Bradley, L. 1990: 'Rhyme, language and children's reading', *Applied Psycholinguistics*, 11, 237–52.
12  See note 5.
13  See note 6.
14  See, for example, Treiman, R. 1985: 'Onsets and rimes as units of spoken syllables: evidence from children', *Journal of Experimental Child Psychology*, 39, 161–81.
15  See, for example, Goswami, U. 1985: 'Children's use of analogy in learning

to read: a developmental study', *Journal of Experimental Child Psychology*, 42, 73–83.

16 Morton, J. 1968: 'Grammar and computation in language behaviour', in J.C. Catford (ed.), *Studies in Language and Language Behaviour*, C.R.L.L.B. Progress Report No. VI, University of Michigan.

17 This idea of a threshold of excitation beyond which the logogen will 'fire' is a feature of early versions of dual-route models, which has been superseded in more recent versions by the idea of interactive activation between levels of features, letters and words (see McClelland, J.L. and Rumelhart, D.E. 1981: 'An interactive activation model of context effects in letter perception: Part 1. An account of basic findings', *Psychological Review*, 88, 375–407). However, 'logogen' (literally translated as 'word producing') can be used to capture the idea of a word recognition device of whatever sort, and for this reason it continues to be a useful term.

18 See Henderson, L. (1982: *Orthography and Word Recognition in Reading*, London: Academic Press, 147–51) for a discussion of this idea.

19 Seymour, P.H.K. and Elder, L. 1986: 'Beginning reading without phonology', *Cognitive Neuropsychology*, 3, 1–37.

20 See note 1.

21 Stuart, M. 1990: 'Factors influencing word recognition in pre-reading children', *British Journal of Psychology*, 81, 135–46.

22 Stuart, M., in press: 'Prediction and qualitative assessment of 5 and 6 year old children's reading: a longitudinal study', *British Journal of Educational Psychology*.

23 Masterson, J., Laxon, V. and Stuart, M. 1992: 'Beginning reading with phonology', *British Journal of Psychology*, 83, 1–12.

# 3

# Cognitive Psychology of Reading Acquisition in the Classroom: Fact or Fantasy?

Philip H.K. Seymour and Henryka M. Evans

*The issues addressed in the previous chapter are here placed firmly in the context of the classroom. In a fictionalized account of a meeting between the academic world of reading research and the teacher involved with teaching the child to read in the classroom, Philip Seymour and Henryka Evans reveal the different perspectives of each world. Apparent differences in the jargon used by each world are shown to address similar objectives, methods and theories. The written words the children experience in different contexts in the classroom provide natural experiments for investigating the differing influences upon learning of both explicit instruction and the child's motivation for learning. The careful recording of children's reading behaviour – the mistakes they make, whether or not the words are sounded out, the size of the sounded out chunks – all provide information about what the child knows about words and the processes the child has available for reading them aloud. All the evidence required by the academic researching reading development is available in the classroom and can be used to guide the teacher's assessment of the reading skills of particular children, once the teachers recognize the significance of the clues before them. The detailed notes to this chapter supply all the additional information necessary to follow up the theoretical issues presented here within the practical world of the classroom.*

## Preamble

The 'psychology of reading' is something which is studied in universities. Academics formulate theories and experiments which purport to describe the ways in which literacy is acquired by children or the processes which occur in the brain of a reader. The 'teaching of reading' is something which happens in classrooms. School teachers make use of reading schemes, activities and inspirations in their effort to encourage the growth of literacy in their classes. Normally these two enterprises proceed quite separately. The 'psychology of reading' is not, as far as we know, an important topic in the curricula of colleges of education or even professional courses in educational psychology. Qualifications or experience in the 'teaching of reading' are seldom found on the CVs of academic researchers.

The question which we would like to consider is whether the gap between the two enterprises might, beneficially, be reduced. We shall approach this by giving a semi-fictionalized account of cognitively motivated research into reading acquisition in a classroom setting. Full details of the research can be obtained by consulting the papers listed in the bibliography. The notes at the end of the chapter provide additional comment and explanation.

## The Lecture Room

Say that one visited a university department in which the 'psychology of reading' was being taught, what would one find? A lecture room, equipped with an overhead projector, a lecturer, whom we will call Dr Lexicon, and a group of students who attend more or less seriously to her words and the diagrams she displays.

'We have talked about "models" of reading,' says Dr Lexicon by way of a summary, 'including the possibility that there are *stages* in literacy development, especially the idea that there is an early stage of *logographic* whole-word recognition based on partial cues, and a later stage of *alphabetic* reading based on knowledge of letters and sounds. This leads eventually to an understanding of the complex *orthographic cipher* underlying English spelling.[1] We also discussed the idea that awareness of speech segments, especially phonemes, might play a critical role in this development. A reading difficulty (or dyslexia) could result from an inability to develop such awareness.[2] Finally, we talked about reading processes and made a distinction between the direct recognition of familiar words and a process of letter–sound translation. We saw how these processes could be studied using lists of real words and lists of unfamiliar nonwords.'[3]

She wished her students good fortune in their examinations. As they drifted out, she switched off the overhead projector and collected up the transparencies she had used in her lecture. Her research assistant, Ms Euphemia Tipperary, filed them neatly into plastic sleeves. 'Do you really think these "models" of reading development would hold good in a real classroom situation?' she asked. 'I mean, can an abstract diagram really convey an accurate or even helpful description of such an individual activity as learning to read? I taught in several schools before I took this job and I can honestly say I'd never heard of reading "models".'[4] 'You think the psychology of reading is too abstract for the classroom?' asked Dr Lexicon. 'Yes, as it stands. But I'm sure that could be changed. Perhaps if the psychologists saw more of what actually happened in the classroom and teachers were given more opportunities to relate research to practice.'

'What do you think I should do?' asked Dr Lexicon humorously. 'Join the beginners when the school restarts after the summer?'

## The Classroom

Suppose we now move to the classroom. The time is early in the autumn term and the new intake of children have been in school for three weeks or so. Dr Lexicon is standing outside the Primary 1 classroom, hand poised to knock. Already she is regretting her decision to spend a day taking a look at the 'chalk-face' of reading. It had seemed a good idea when it was proposed three months previously – now she isn't so sure. Away from her lecture room, theories and models, she is feeling rather like a new entrant herself.

The noise emanating from behind the door labelled 'Primary 1 – Mrs Cramond' is daunting to say the least. And surely all these pegs with their individual pictures and clearly written names do not belong to just one class?

Dr Lexicon reproves herself for prevaricating and knocks firmly on the door just as the hubbub within ceases abruptly. After a second or two the door swings open revealing a small boy wearing a policeman's hat several sizes too large. He seems to be content to stand staring until joined by an even smaller girl, who announces: 'Mrs Cramond's doing the dinners'.

As three more children join the two at the door Mrs Cramond is alerted to the fact that her visitor has arrived. Wondering what had possessed her to agree to having a psychologist from the University in her classroom, she hurries to the door and invites Dr Lexicon in. 'I'm sorry I didn't hear your knock. It takes a few minutes for them to settle down when they first come in. Daniel, Paula! Come and sit down. This is our visitor, Dr Lexicon, who has come to watch us doing all our activities. She knows all about how children learn to read and we'll be showing her our reading books later on. First we'll have "News Time".'

As the children clamour to tell their 'news' to the rather flustered Mrs Cramond, Dr Lexicon is gazing around the classroom. She had not expected such a wealth of print. Everything seems to bear a label. Sets of stacked sliding trays are presumably holding the children's work. Each is labelled with the child's name. The walls are covered in paintings, all with appropriate print – 'My mummy', 'This is my rabbit', 'Dad is in the garden'. A large poster charts the weather, the movable pointer indicating 'sunny', 'windy', 'rainy', 'foggy' etc. The 'days of the week' adorn a further wall while a cheerful rainbow supplies the background for the colour names. Underneath, the numerals 1–10 appear with the printed form of the name and the appropriate number of objects. All the games and activities are labelled either with single words, 'jigsaws', 'Lego', 'paints', 'sand', or with phrases, 'Only four in the Wendy house', 'Library corner, Quiet please!', 'These are our gerbils, Tom and Gerry'. A colourful alphabet frieze depicts the lower case letters alongside appropriate pictures.

'I was just saying,' interrupts Mrs Cramond, 'if you'd like to take a seat, I'm about to hear the "Giraffes".' Somewhat mystified

Dr Lexicon lowers herself onto a tiny chair while a group of five or six children crowd around holding brightly coloured reading books. 'We'll look at our words first,' says Mrs Cramond briskly. 'Let's see if you can remember who this is.' She holds up a flashcard. 'Ben,' choruses the group. 'And what did Ben do?' She holds up a second card. 'Jump!' 'And what does this word say?' 'Dog.' The 'Giraffes' are obviously adept at recognizing the dozen or so flashcards presented by their teacher. Mrs Cramond spreads the cards on the table and asks individual children in turn to find a particular card. 'Let's make a story now', she says. 'Who can find three cards to put on the wall? All right, Paula, you come and choose. "Ben", "can", "jump". Very good. Let's put Paula's story on the wall. Stuart, you come and point to the bit that says "Ben". That's right. Now where is "jump" . . . ?'

The lesson with the 'Giraffes' finishes with each child reading aloud from his or her reading book. Mrs Cramond points out mistakes, elicits correct answers, praises extravagantly and reads over the pages for the next day. One new word is encountered – 'bump'. This is written on the blackboard and a new flashcard is made. 'Does it look like another word we know?' asks Mrs Cramond. 'Bump your head,' announces the miniature policeman. 'You're telling me a story about "bump", Daniel,' says Mrs Cramond. 'Just look at the word. Does it look like a word on another card?' 'It's a bit like "jump",' volunteers the small girl called Paula. 'Well done, Paula. Can you see that, everybody? Here is "jump" and this is "bump".' 'Bump-jump, bump-jump,' chants Daniel, 'that makes a rhyme Mrs Cramond.' 'Bump-jump, bump-jump,' the others join in. 'That's enough now,' says Mrs Cramond. 'Back to your seats and draw me a picture of Ben getting the bump on his head.'

'They seem a bright lot,' remarks Dr Lexicon, gingerly easing herself out of the infant-sized chair. 'Oh, the "Giraffes" are my most advanced group,' Mrs Cramond replies. The "Elephants" are not so far on in word recognition and the "Tigers" have not started formal reading as yet. They are working on word and picture matching games.'

'You seem to be concentrating on logographic reading,' says Dr Lexicon. 'What do you mean?' asks Mrs Cramond. 'You are teaching whole words. The children are developing word identification skills. Most reading theorists believe that this is the first stage in beginning reading. This is followed by the alphabetic stage when children learn grapheme–phoneme correspondences and how to analyse print. I expect your class will reach this stage towards the end of the year.'

'Do you mean my phonic programme?' asks Mrs Cramond cautiously. 'I've started that already.' She gestures to the corner of the room. 'Take a look. I'm going to hear the "Elephants" now.'

Dr Lexicon walks over to examine the display. A large letter 'S' is pinned to the wall. Surrounding it are pictures of a bright yellow sun, a sock, a sausage and a snake. Underneath, on a table draped with a blue cloth, is a collection of objects – a plastic soldier, a school-bag, a sandal, a saucer, a packet of salt, a stone, some sellotape, and a pair of scissors. 'This is our sound table,' announces a voice by her side. It is Daniel of the policeman's hat. 'I brought the soldier.' 'And I brought the sandal,' adds Paula, who seems to follow wherever Daniel goes. 'That's because we're doing "sss" this week and you have to put things on the table that begin with "sss"'. 'I can draw "sss"', interrupts Daniel. 'I've got it in my workbook and I can make "sss" with plasticine. It's easy because its just like a snake.'

Mrs Cramond is again busy calling the children together. They all gather round the piano with an assortment of instruments, xylophones, bells, drums and shakers. 'Let's make some word tunes,' she says. 'If you don't have an instrument clap your hands. Can anyone think of a nice big word to start off?' 'Elephant!' 'All right, Nicola. We'll all clap Nicola's word. Everybody together. El-e-phant, el-e-phant!' The children beat out the rhythm with surprising accuracy as they chant in chorus.

'I see you devote time to fostering phonological awareness,' remarks Dr Lexicon as the children collect workbooks, pencils and crayons from their trays. 'I'm sure I don't know about that,' replies Mrs Cramond. 'Would you like to go round and watch the children work?' she says. 'You must be stiff sitting on that chair.' 'Not at all.' Dr Lexicon eases herself to her feet with a grimace.

The 'Giraffes' are busy with phonic workbooks, ringing and colouring all the objects on the page which begin with 's'. The 'Elephants' are writing 'stories' in their language jotters finding words they need in the 'Word Bank'. Mrs Cramond is kept busy writing out new words when requested. The 'Tigers' are playing word matching games based on lotto, snap and dominoes.

'Do you know what this says?' asks Dr Lexicon as one of the group matches 'big' to its partner. 'No, I'm a "Tiger" ', says the child with an air of having explained all. 'I can tell you,' says Emma, one of the 'Elephants'. 'It's "dog", we have "dog" in our book.' 'How do you know it says "dog"?' asks Dr Lexicon. 'Because there's its long waggy tail,' answers the child, pointing to the descender of the 'g'. Daniel, in hat, and with Paula in tow, is passing on his way to Mrs Cramond's desk. 'Do you know this word, Daniel?' asks the psychologist. Daniel looks at the domino. 'It's not "dog" ', he says, 'I know "dog". That's a "b" and that's an "i", and a "g". It's "big"!'

## The Research

Dr Lexicon has been given a great deal to think about during her morning visit and an idea has taken root in her mind. Before leaving she broaches the subject with the teacher. Would Mrs Cramond allow Dr Lexicon to carry out a study of the literacy development of the children during the first school year?

Mrs Cramond seems a little hesitant. There have been so many arguments about the teaching of reading in recent years and she is worried that she may not be doing the right thing. Dr Lexicon assures her that she has found the work going on in the classroom extremely interesting. 'It seems to me that you are developing the dual processes in parallel,' she explains, 'rather than focusing on the logographic process initially and moving on to the alphabetic stage at a later point.[5] It is also appears that you are seeking to develop phonological awareness of large speech segments, such as syllables or rhymes.'[6]

'It all sounds very technical,' says Mrs Cramond doubtfully. 'How often would you want to come? I wouldn't want the children's work disrupted too much. At this age they are so easily distracted.'

'It would be my assistant, Euphemia Tipperary, who would come,' Dr Lexicon assures her. 'Probably once a week if that's agreeable. Euphemia was a primary teacher for several years before she started in research and I'm sure she would fit in and get on well with the children.'

Mrs Cramond, now intrigued by the idea, says she would be happy to participate if Dr Lexicon will approach the Headmaster, Mr McHugh, for his permission. A final detail is the necessity for a quiet area where the research can be set up. This is available next to the classroom in the form of a large storeroom equipped with power points which will be needed later when the reading tasks will be transferred to a computer. This settled, Dr Lexicon hurries off to explain the project to the Headteacher before returning to the University to deliver an introductory lecture on the 'psychology of reading' to the new student intake.

Dr Lexicon and her assistant, the engaging Ms Tipperary, then undertake an extended series of discussions about the questions which should be tackled in the research and the methods which should be used. From these debates it becomes evident that Dr Lexicon's primary interest is in the cognitive processes[7] which develop as the children learn to read and the way these relate to currently formulated theories of reading acquisition. In essence, there appear to be three distinct processes which interest her, to which she applies the terms 'logographic', 'alphabetic' and 'phonological'. She thinks these terms refer to functions or activities which occur in the brains of children as they learn to read and which support the later establishment of more sophisticated processes which she characterizes as 'orthographic'.

*Logographic process*   The first process concerns the capacity to recognize and identify familiar words. It approximates the classroom 'whole word' method or 'look-and-say' strategy of early instruction. Dr Lexicon calls this the 'logographic process' because it resembles the way that the Chinese read their complex characters (or 'logographs'). Each logograph stands for a whole word and does not contain any systematic clues as to its pronunciation. Our numerals, 1, 2, 3, 4, and symbols such as £, & and % are logographs in this sense.[8]

*Alphabetic process*   The second process is implicated in an ability to work out a pronunciation for an unfamiliar word. It relates to the practice of linking letters to their sounds or the 'phonic' aspects of classroom instruction. Dr Lexicon refers to this as the 'alphabetic process' because alphabetic writing systems are based on a correspondence between individual symbols (the letters of the alphabet) and the individual vowel and consonant sounds from which speech is composed.[9]

*Phonological process*   The third process is concerned with the speech side of the correspondence between letters and sounds. The argument here is that, in order to read an alphabetic script, a child needs to understand that words can be broken down into a sequence of elementary 'sounds'. These sound sequences must be held in memory and reassembled as fluent speech. Dr Lexicon uses the term 'phonological' to refer to these processes because phonology is the branch of linguistics which is specifically concerned with the sound structure of speech.[10]

Thus, Dr Lexicon's hypothesis is that the activity going on in the Primary 1 classroom, although seemingly integrated and indivisible, has a psychological, or 'cognitive', effect which can be described in terms of the formation of three distinct processes or functions. In order to investigate this idea she and her assistant, Euphemia Tipperary, will need to devise a set of experimental procedures which they can use to gain information about the logographic, alphabetic and phonological processes. If she is to trace the development of the processes over time she will need to apply the procedures at intervals, that is, she will need to carry out a *longitudinal* study.

   In the remainder of the discussion we will outline the procedures which were applied, describe a few of the results which were obtained and participate in a debate about some theoretical and educational implications.

## Some Results

The research proceeded throughout the whole of the first school year. Regularly, week by week, Euphemia Tipperary arrived at the school in her battered VW Golf and took up position in her 'cupboard' adjacent to the classroom. The children visited her individually for brief sessions – generally no more than ten to fifteen minutes – in which brief tasks were carried out. She fitted in well with the school routine and the children enjoyed and looked forward to their contacts with her.

During the year large amounts of data were collected. At a most general level these results confirmed that progress was being made. The children steadily improved in their ability to read the words they were being taught, to tackle new words and to carry out phonological tasks. It was also true that this progress was somewhat uneven and that some children seemed to move ahead rapidly while others lagged behind.

As we have already noted, Dr Lexicon's goal was to monitor the development of three distinct processes – the logographic, alphabetic and phonological processes. Each of these processes had associated with it a particular set of procedures which Euphemia carried out with the individual children. Accordingly, we will divide the description of the study into three sections, one for each of the target processes.

## The logographic process

The logographic process is defined as a procedure for recognition of familiar words which is normally available to children from the earliest stages of their reading development. Some theorists insist that the term should be restricted to reading which is strictly *visual*, such as the identification of 'dog' by its 'waggy tail'. Others, Dr Lexicon included, would extend the term to any process which is restricted to the identification of the members of a set of familiar words and which does not generalize to the identification of new or unfamiliar words.[11]

The logographic process was examined by observing the children's performance when they attempted to identify words taken from their reading scheme or words which were otherwise available in the classroom. The words were presented individually on flashcards, in lower case letters, without supporting context. Ms

Tipperary made a note of the responses which were given, whether or not 'sounding' occurred, and whether the response was correct, an error or a refusal (a 'don't know' response). There was no strong evidence of a spontaneous adoption of visual identification strategies. Some children commented on the 'waggy tail' of 'dog' and the 'two eyes' of 'look' but these were specific points which had been emphasized by Mrs Cramond in her teaching. Hence, the logographic process was defined solely in terms of the response pattern shown by a child. The main features of this pattern are, first, that correct responses occur only to words which are already familiar, second that unfamiliar words are likely to be refused, and third that, where errors occur, they are typically words drawn from among already familiar items which share one or more letters (or an aspect of meaning) with the target.[12]

As an illustration of logographic reading we can refer to the pattern of responses made by Emma, one of the middle ability 'Elephants', when she was asked to read words from the reading scheme during week 6 of the first term. Out of twenty-one items she read nine correctly, refused six, and made word substitutions on six others (you-'yes', come-'can', help-'look', where-'here', no-'yes', I-'you'). Four of these errors share common letters. Two of them are possibly linked by meaning. All of them were drawn from Emma's 'reading set' of familiar words. There was no evidence of 'sounding' of letters.

One important question is whether logographic reading develops 'naturally', so that children effortlessly acquire words they encounter in their environments rather as an infant acquires speech, or whether some formal instruction, based on flashcards and reading books, is necessary. Dr Lexicon considered that Mrs Cramond's classroom presented a good opportunity for examining this question. It appeared that there was one set of words deriving from the Ginn 360 reading scheme which Mrs Cramond was actively attempting to teach. We will call this set the 'book vocabulary'. Then there were numerous other words which were meaningfully displayed around the classroom but which were not promoted by teaching (names of colours, objects, toys etc.). These can be referred to as the 'room vocabulary'. Finally, there were the children's first names which adorned their pictures, workbooks, worktrays and cloakroom pegs. If logographic acquisition is 'natural' it could be anticipated that the children should learn room words and names no less effectively than their book words.

In order to test this expectation Euphemia Tipperary asked the children to attempt to read room words and names as well as book words. A striking finding was that the children appeared to have developed very little familiarity with the room words. Thus, when Emma was shown sixteen room words in week 7 of term 1, she made thirteen refusals and three word substitutions (one-'not', purple-'help', eight-'elephant'). The first two responses were drawn from the book vocabulary and the third from the alphabet frieze. In week 9, when shown a second list of fifteen room words, she refused fourteen and referred to 'book' as a 'funny kind of "look" '. The treatment of room words as essentially unfamiliar was typical of the class as a whole at this stage.

This result suggests that logographic reading is not a natural development. However, results for reading of the class names suggested a quite opposite conclusion. When the names were shown on flash cards the children almost all displayed a remarkable facility for reading them. By the end of term 1 just over half the class were able to identify all of the names without error. By the end of term 2 there was only one child who still made occasional errors. In contrast, only four children read any 'room words' at the end of term 1, and, with one or two exceptions, performance remained poor during term 2. The names were never emphasized in formal teaching by Mrs Cramond. Thus, it seems that their acquisition was a 'natural' (untaught) process. Presumably, the point of importance is that the names possessed a functional significance and inherent interest for the children which the 'room words' clearly lacked.[13]

Dr Lexicon concluded that a logographic process of word recognition was formed by each of the children during the Primary 1 school year. The process encompassed only words which had been taught by Mrs Cramond (the 'book words') or items which had attracted interest and attention (the 'names'). It appeared that recognition often depended on a few details of each word, such as the presence of specific letters, rather than on the overall structure or shape.[14] The children appeared to possess a memory for the words included in their reading vocabulary and typically selected their responses from this set.[15]

## The alphabetic process

The alphabetic process is a procedure by which a knowledge of letter–sound associations is used to assist in the reading or writing of unfamiliar words. One essential requirement is that the children should know the letters and their sounds.[16] The other is that they should be able to apply this knowledge. In reading, this might involve finding the sounds for each of the letters in proper left-to-right sequence and then 'blending' the sounds to construct a pronunciation. For spelling, it could involve breaking a word up into its elementary sounds and then selecting and writing a letter corresponding to each sound.[17]

In order to assess the availability of the alphabetic process it is necessary to present the children with items which are genuinely *unfamiliar*. A standard approach is to construct made-up words, called 'nonwords'. These could be simple items (e.g. han, mip, zug) or more complex forms created by rearranging the elements of real words. Thus, Dr Lexicon and Ms Tipperary constructed two sets of nonwords, one based on the 'book vocabulary' and the other on the children's names. Elements of words such as 'dog', 'jump' and 'help' were recombined to produce nonwords such as 'heg', 'julp' and 'domp'. A similar approach was followed in the construction of 'non-names', e.g. 'Nicola' and 'Richard' yielded the non-names 'Nicard' and 'Richola'. The items were written on flashcards for presentation to the children.[18]

Basic letter-sound knowledge was acquired very rapidly. By the end of term 1 there were four children who knew all of the letters. By the middle of term 2 all children (bar one) could identify and write all twenty-six letters. In the early stages children were often able to relate letters to words even though they could not articulate the 'sound' of the letter. For example, in one early attempt Emma gave only five correct letter sounds but was able to give some information about fourteen other letters. This was sometimes a word which began with the sound of the letter (e.g. 's' – 'snake'). On other occasions it was a letter contained in a word, e.g. 'k' – 'that's at the end of "look" '; 'y' – 'my brother Ryan'. It should perhaps be emphasized that the children learned to associate the letters with 'sound names', such as 'b' – 'buh', 's' – 'sss', and not with their conventional names, 'bee' and 'ess'.[19]

# 74 P.H.K. Seymour and H.M. Evans

*Table 3.1* Responses by four children to twenty nonwords

| Child | Trial | 'Logographic' | | 'Alphabetic' | | |
|---|---|---|---|---|---|---|
| | | Refusal | Word error | Sounded (no blend) | Nonword error | Correct response |
| Nicola | 1 | 1 | 18 | 1 | 0 | 0 |
| | 2 | 0 | 1 | 3 | 7 | 9 |
| | 3 | 0 | 4 | 0 | 4 | 12 |
| Jennifer | 1 | 19 | 0 | 0 | 1 | 0 |
| | 2 | 0 | 3 | 2 | 8 | 7 |
| | 3 | 0 | 1 | 0 | 4 | 15 |
| Richard | 1 | 9 | 5 | 0 | 5 | 1 |
| | 2 | 0 | 9 | 1 | 7 | 3 |
| | 3 | 0 | 0 | 0 | 5 | 15 |
| Gillian | 1 | 20 | 0 | 0 | 0 | 0 |
| | 2 | 1 | 2 | 12 | 1 | 4 |
| | 3 | 0 | 2 | 2 | 4 | 12 |

Trials 1 and 2 occurred during term 1, and trial 3 during term 2. Refusals and word substitutions have been viewed as typically 'logographic' responses. Soundings (without a blend), nonword errors and correct responses are viewed as indications of 'alphabetic' reading.

The emergence of the alphabetic process is marked in various ways. The most obvious of these is the advance in success in pronouncing unfamiliar nonwords. Another is the occurrence of overt 'sounding' of letters.[20] Finally, there is the error pattern. It is expected that a proportion of the errors generated by the alphabetic process will be nonwords.[21]

We can see this happening in the results produced by four of the children towards the end of term 1 and at the beginning of term 2. Table 3.1 gives a breakdown of responses to unfamiliar nonwords by Nicola, Jennifer, Richard and Gillian during this period. At the first test point the children were unable to read the nonwords. They responded by saying 'don't know' (Jennifer and Gillian) or by substituting a word (Nicola) or by a combination of refusals and word substitutions. This pattern is typical of a pre-alphabetic logographic approach. By the second test, held at the end of term 1, the children no longer refused to respond and a proportion of responses gave evidence of alphabetic processing. These included 'sounding' of individual letters without synthesis of a response (Gillian), production of incorrect nonword responses (Nicola, Jennifer and Richard) and production of some correct responses. At the time of the third test, early in term 2, all four children were producing appreciable numbers of correct responses to nonwords.

The occurrence of audible (or visible) 'sounding' of letters was a clear hallmark of alphabetic reading. Sounding was a predominant feature of the attempts at nonword reading but was much less evident when familiar words were presented. Thus, attempts at reading non-names ('Nicard' etc.) were accompanied by extensive sounding which was entirely absent when the names themselves were read. A strategy change in attempts to read the 'room words' was also apparent. As has been noted, these words, though on public display, were largely unfamiliar. In term 2 the refusals and word substitutions were replaced by relentless sounding of letters. As a consequence of the complex and irregular spellings contained in many of the words the children were typically unable to convert the sounds to a satisfactory blend. For example, 'two' was sounded as 't', 'w', 'o', and read as 'twau', and 'eight' was sounded as 'e', 'i', 'g', 'h', 't', and read as 'egt'.[22]

From these results, Dr Lexicon concluded that all of the children developed an alphabetic process during their first school year. They learned to equate letters with sounds and to use this knowledge when attempting to read or write unfamiliar words or nonwords. Some theorists have suggested that alphabetic writing is a more natural process than alphabetic reading. This is because the division of a word into its elementary sounds and the selection of a letter to correspond to each sound fits well with the necessarily sequential production of writing. If this proposal was correct it would be anticipated that the children should learn to write nonwords more easily or sooner than they learn to read them.[23] A difference in favour of nonword writing was shown by some of the children during the first school term. Thereafter, most children scored higher on nonword reading than on nonword writing.

## The phonological process

The phonological process is a procedure for division of speech into its component segments and for the retention and manipulation of these segments in memory. This is held to be critical for literacy development because a grasp of the alphabetic aspect of writing depends on a capacity to perceive that words are made up out of sequences of 'sounds' which relate in a systematic way to the letters used to spell them. The question which interested Dr Lexicon concerned the nature of the units of sound which might be important. On the one hand, she had noted that the phonic activities encouraged by Mrs Cramond appeared to emphasize links between individual letters and their sounds. At the same time, there appeared to be many other activities which emphasized the division of words into syllables and into rhymes and alliterations. On theoretical grounds it had been suggested that division of words into a beginning and a rhyming end might be an easier and developmentally earlier achievement for children than the division of words into the individual elements which correspond to the letters. To illustrate, it is thought that it might be easier for children to appreciate that 'sprint' and 'flint' share a common rhyme, or that 'sprint' and 'sprawl' share a common beginning, than that 'sprint' is composed of the sequence 's'+'p'+'r'+'i'+'n'+'t'.[24]

In order to find out which of these levels was the more important Dr Lexicon made use of a 'segmentation task'. It should be emphasized that this was a 'phonological' task, based entirely on *spoken* words and their component sounds. No written words were involved. Euphemia Tipperary devised a simple game which she could play with the children. She presented them with a small creature who was described as an alien who had landed on Earth and who was trying to learn the language. He could say some words but only if he broke them up into parts. The number of parts varied, being two on one occasion, three on another and three or more on another. In the first part of the game Euphemia spoke for the alien and the child was invited to guess the word he was trying to say. This procedure assesses a child's capacity to recombine or *blend* segments of speech. Following this phase, the child was invited to take the part of the alien and say words suggested by Euphemia in 2, 3 or 3+ bits. This procedure assesses a capacity to *segment* speech.[25]

Early in the Primary 1 year the children had some success in blending, especially for the shorter sequences, but were quite unable to cope with segmentation. Their responses included refusals, repetition of the target, or production of rhymes or associations. Segmentation ability emerged gradually as the year advanced. By the third term many of the children were able to produce segmented responses containing the instructed number of parts. These responses were classified according to whether or not they involved divisions at the theoretically appropriate points. Thus, for segmentation into two parts, the expected division is between the initial consonants and the rhyme, so that 'sprint' = 'spr' + 'int'. Other two-way divisions, such as 'sp' + 'rint', 'spri' + 'nt', 'sprin' + 't' etc. depart from this expectation. The analysis of the data suggested that the children developed a good grasp of the division of words into many parts during the year (e.g. 'sprint' = 's' + 'p' + 'r' + 'i' + 'n' + 't') but that they lacked a strong commitment to the initial consonant + rhyme division in two-part segmentation.[26]

On these grounds, Dr Lexicon concluded that the children developed a phonological process for segmentation and recombination of speech during their first school year. This process appeared to be directed towards division of words into small parts corresponding to letters rather than into larger parts based on the rhyme.

## The Model

During the summer Dr Lexicon and her assistant Ms Tipperary reviewed the results of the research and discussed their theoretical implications. It was Dr Lexicon's hope that the outcomes of the study might help her to formulate a new 'model' of the process of literacy acquisition.

One issue was whether the study had demonstrated the existence of two distinct processes in early reading – the 'logographic' and 'alphabetic' processes. Dr Lexicon thought that the processes were satisfactorily distinguished on the basis of their error patterns, especially the predominance of refusals and word substitutions in logographic reading and the production of nonword responses in alphabetic reading. Ms Tipperary thought that the occurrence of 'sounding' was the clearest indication of the alphabetic process. Another issue was whether the processes developed concurrently or in succession. There was evidence that alphabetic reading emerged somewhat later than logographic reading. On the other hand it did not appear to be the case that the logographic process was then abandoned. Euphemia said that it was her strong impression that the children persisted with logogaphic recognition of familiar words during the period when they were making extensive use of alphabetic procedures to read unfamiliar words. For example, the first names were read without sounding at a time when the non-names almost always provoked sounding.[27] It was her opinion that the timing of appearance of the alphabetic process depended very much on the teaching approach which was adopted. The alphabetic process appeared later because time was needed to teach the children about the letters of the alphabet and their sounds.[28]

'One question', said Dr Lexicon, 'is whether these two processes will continue in the future, so that more advanced reading is also based on two functions, as suggested by the dual-route model.'[29]

Ms Tipperary agreed that this was an important question. 'It will be difficult to investigate', she said. 'Say we carried on with the study into the second school year. I think we would find that words and nonwords started to produce similar error patterns, with a mixture of word and nonword substitutions. Also, I think we would find that sounding of letters disappeared. I could see this happening already in some of the children.'[30]

Dr Lexicon thought it would be very worthwhile to continue the study into the second year. One possibility, she said, might be to take the computer into the school. The words and nonwords could be presented on the computer screen. A voice switch could be used to detect the onset of speech and the computer could measure the vocal reaction times for pronouncing words or nonwords. If the underlying processes were different the reaction time patterns might show different characteristics. Logographic responses to familiar words might appear relatively fast and would be unaffected by the number of letters in the word. Alphabetic responses to unfamiliar nonwords would depend on letter-by-letter processing and should be slower and also affected by the number of letters which needed to be translated.[31] 'It is my expectation', she said, 'that, using this reaction time method, we might see the logographic and alphabetic processes surviving as distinct functions through most of the second school year. Nonetheless, I think they might have vanished and been replaced by some more advanced process by the third year.'[32]

On the basis of these speculations, Dr Lexicon proposed a theory of literacy acquisition. She called this a 'dual foundation model' of development. The essential idea was that the 'logographic process' and the 'alphabetic process' are twin functions which develop in parallel during the early period of acquisition and which act as essential *foundations* for the formation of a later and more sophisticated 'orthographic process'.[33] In order to pursue this idea it would be vital to continue the longitudinal study into the second school year and beyond. She decided to write to the Headteacher, Mr McHugh, therefore, to ask if this would be possible.

## The Implications

Mr McHugh replied that he would be pleased to consider an extension of the study but that before deciding he would like to arrange a meeting at which Dr Lexicon could explain to him and his staff what exactly the research had involved and what might be the implications for the work going on in the school. This meeting was held shortly before the start of the new school year. Dr Lexicon and Ms Tipperary met with the school staff and a few other interested parties and gave an outline description of the research method, some of the findings and the 'dual foundation' theory. The meeting was then thrown open for discussion.

Mr McHugh said that the research sounded very interesting. From his point of view, the important question was whether the school was approaching the teaching of reading in the best possible way. Dr Lexicon had spoken about a 'theory' of literacy acquisition. He wanted to know if the school's 'educational theory' could be improved, and, if so, how?

Mrs Cramond interjected at this point. She said that she had found the research very interesting and that the children had really enjoyed Euphemia's visits. But she was puzzled about all this talk about theories and models and processes. Her approach to teaching reading was one she had learned from the infant mistress when she took her first teaching job after finishing training. The ideas of starting with a particular vocabulary and with the letters and their 'sound names' had all been used successfully by this older teacher.

Another lady, apparently not a member of the school staff, asked if she could make a point. She said that Mrs Cramond's methods sounded to her rather old-fashioned and traditional. She had recently attended several very interesting seminars at which it was being argued that the important thing was to emphasize the value of reading and writing as forms of communication and transmission of meaning. She thought that techniques involving flashcards, word banks and letter-sound learning were alien to this new and more exciting approach and should be abandoned forthwith.[34]

Mrs Cramond turned pink and began to mutter angrily. Mr McHugh glanced at her, entreating calm, and asked Dr Lexicon if she would like to comment.

'Well,' said Dr Lexicon, 'I agree of course that it is important that children should find reading and writing interesting and exciting and that they should realize that written words are an important form of communication. But I think it would be wrong to imagine that what I have called the 'foundations', that is, the formation of a logographic vocabulary and a grasp of the alphabetic principle, are in any way in conflict with this goal. Certainly, I think it would be a bad mistake to try to remove the foundation processes. In order for later development to occur it is essential that children should internalize some vocabulary and that they should acquire a knowledge of letter–sound links. Although some of this might be picked up incidentally, rather as occurred with the class names in our study, I am sure that the most efficient approach is to set out to teach a specific vocabulary, as was done by Mrs Cramond.'[35]

'Could I chip in here?' asked Euphemia. 'I agree with every-thing that Dr Lexicon has said. One thing which was very evident was that the children did not naturally acquire the words which were on display around the classroom. But I do have to say that the book vocabulary which was taught seemed to me to be a very poor one consisting of a very dull and uninteresting set of words. Building up the logographic foundation would be much better served by using a more colourful and meaningful vocabulary.'[36]

'One point I was not quite sure about', said Mr McHugh, 'was this reference to what you called the phonological process. Is this something we should be trying to teach? And, if so, how?'[37]

Dr Lexicon replied that there was good evidence to support the conclusion that phonological processes were significantly involved in literacy development. She had noted that Mrs Cramond en-couraged various activities which involved dividing words into syllables or pointing out similarities between words which rhymed. All this surely helped children to appreciate that words could be segmented into component sounds.[38] None the less, it was her view that the most effective way of developing the 'phonological awareness' necessary for reading and spelling was through teach-ing about letters and letter groups with an emphasis on their pho-nological equivalents. She thought that this was why the children had learned to divide words into sequences of elementary sounds. This approach was consistent with the emphasis on letter-sound learning and the 'sounding out' which had appeared to be the characteristic feature of the alphabetic process.[39]

'I am still not quite clear about this,' said Mr McHugh. 'Does that mean that the work with syllables and rhymes is irrelevant?'

'No, I don't think so,' said Dr Lexicon. 'It is true that at the foundation stage it does seem to be the case that letter–sound equivalences are important. However, at a later point, when an orthographic lexicon is being formed, it may well be true that these larger phonological structures, such as syllables or rhymes, become important as a basis for organization of words into a coherent structure or framework.'[40]

Another member of the group interrupted at this point, saying that she was a teacher in the school who took responsibility for the Primary 3 year. 'All of this is very interesting to me,' she said. 'You have talked about "foundation processes" and more advanced "orthographic" processes. I would like to know when the "foundation" stage ends and the "orthographic" stage begins. And I would like to know what we need to do in order to assist orthographic development.'

Dr Lexicon agreed that these were very important questions. Indeed, one of her main reasons for raising the possibility of continuing with the study was precisely in order to attempt to map out the transition from a 'foundation' to an 'orthographic' level. 'My present idea', she said, 'is that formation of the two foundation processes probably predominates throughout the greater part of the first two primary years. During this time the children build up a basic store of word knowledge and an alphabetic procedure for letter–sound translation. However, these two processes are not in themselves adequate for reading and writing English. The logographic approach to word learning is inefficient on account of the very large number of individual words which must be acquired. The alphabetic approach is inadequate because English contains numerous complex and irregular structures which cannot be unravelled by converting individual letters to sounds. Thus, although the "logographic" and "alphabetic" processes are a natural initial approach to reading and spelling, they have to give way to a better adapted procedure. I would see this as happening from the Primary 3 year onwards.'[41]

'Good,' said the Primary 3 teacher, 'but that brings me back to the other part of my question – how can we assist what you called "orthographic" development?'

'My impression', said Euphemia Tipperary, 'is that it is an almost automatic process. Orthographic development involves coming to terms with a very complicated spelling system in which sounds are inconsistently related to letters and letter groups. I think teachers do a certain amount of work with digraphs, consonant clusters, vowel groups, and so forth, but that they don't set out to teach the whole system bit by bit.'

'Yes, that is my view also,' said Dr Lexicon. 'Provided that the logographic and alphabetic foundations are adequately established, that there is a capability for phonological segmentation, and that children gain plenty of experience in relating text to speech, then I think that a process of internalization of the orthographic structure will occur automatically, leading in due course to a fully developed and sophisticated reader.'[42]

'I am not sure about that,' interjected a bespectacled young man. 'I am in charge of the Primary 4 class. I agree that most of the children seem to be dealing with complex print, reading for comprehension, and so on. None the less, I have some children in the class who seem to be having real problems.'

'Also in Primary 3,' said that Primary 3 teacher. 'I had at least two children last year who seemed to make very little progress.'

Mr McHugh said that there were several children in the middle and upper primary years who were causing concern. They seemed not to be making good progress in reading despite well-intentioned efforts on the part of the staff. In some instances it had been necessary to consult the educational psychologists and the learning support service. Some parents were becoming very agitated and were mentioning terms such as 'dyslexia'[43] and demanding that special treatment programmes should be arranged. Mr McHugh would be very interested to know how these cases of reading difficulty fitted into Dr Lexicon's theories.

Dr Lexicon replied that it was well known that a proportion of children did not develop literacy easily or normally. The cause was a mystery, but might be linked to genetics or to other factors which influenced the early development of the brain.[44] In her terms, the characteristic of these children was that the 'orthographic system' did not develop normally or automatically, as in other children.

'What we really want to know', interrupted Mr McHugh, 'is what we should do about it.'

'It is a complicated issue', said Dr Lexicon. 'In order to examine it I think I would want to make a distinction between a foundation level of development and a more advanced, orthographic, level. It is my suspicion that children with difficulties whose reading age is below about 7 years will be found to lack one or both of the foundation processes. This could be investigated using methods similar to those which we employed with the Primary 1 class. We would assess word knowledge, letter-sound knowledge and ability to read simple nonwords. It is my expectation that we would find that the children differed in the focus of their difficulty, so that some had a "logographic" problem, affecting the learning of a word set, while others had an "alphabetic" problem affecting phonological awareness and the application of letter-sound knowledge.'[45]

'Once we had found which aspect was affected', said Euphemia Tipperary, 'we could direct teaching accordingly, and work towards the establishment of the foundation processes.'[46]

Dr Lexicon added that many children with difficulties might already have proceeded beyond the foundation stage. The investigation of their problems would require new methods which probed the development of an orthographic system. Probably these methods would also rely on the contrast between real words and nonwords. Again, it was her expectation that the children would differ in the nature of their disability, some having special problems with words, others with nonwords.[47]

## Postscript

Mr McHugh thanked Dr Lexicon for her presentation. He said that he had found the discussion very interesting and that, for his part, he would be pleased for the investigation to continue so that the more advanced levels of reading development could be studied. He also thought that it would be very helpful to have more information about the children with reading difficulties. He looked enquiringly at the members of his staff who nodded their agreement.[48]

Dr Lexicon thanked him and said that she and her assistant were very much looking forward to continuing with the research. The co-operation of the school and the staff was greatly appreciated. At present, the situation seemed to be one in which cognitive researchers were seeking the support of schools for permission to pursue studies which were mainly theoretical or academic in their impact. It was her hope that this situation might change in the future and that schools might call on researchers to assist their understanding of the cognitive effects of their teaching, both in general and in the cases of reading disability.

# NOTES

1   This account of literacy development derives from the work of Gough and Hillinger (1980), Marsh et al. (1981), Frith (1985) and Ehri (1992).

2   An important conclusion from recent research on reading acquisition has been that a child's capacity to reflect on the segmental structure of his or her own speech may be critical. Goswami and Bryant (1990) have provided a helpful discussion.

3   A recurring theme in the cognitive psychology and cognitive neuro-psychology of reading has been the suggestion that literacy is supported by two functionally distinct processes, a *lexical* process which is specialized for identification of words, and a *non-lexical* process which deals with graph-eme–phoneme correspondences (letter–sound associations). It is argued the lexical process is necessary because many English words have irregular spellings. The non-lexical process is necessary because people are able to read unfamiliar words or nonwords which are not represented in a lexical system. Lists of words of varying regularity and nonwords have commonly been used to study these two processes. Ellis (1984) provides a good intro-ductory account.

4   A 'model' is a theoretical account which purports to describe abstract fea-tures of the reading process. Some models refer mainly to the structural organization, or 'cognitive architecture', of orthographic (reading and spell-ing) functions and other functions (e.g. speech and meaning). Other models deal with the process of development, especially the causes of progress and the strategies deployed at different stages. Models can be represented ver-bally or diagrammatically or as a working system embodied in a computer program.

5   A common feature of the developmental models (e.g. Frith, 1985) is that the logographic, alphabetic and orthographic stages occur in strict succession.

6   A standard view has been that mastery of the alphabetic principle depends on access to abstract units of speech called *phonemes*. These are small units consisting of the individual vowels and consonants from which speech is composed. Goswami and Bryant (1990) questioned this view and argued that larger units, especially those involved in *rhymes*, were important.

7   A *cognitive process* is an abstract function which is carried out by the brain. It may involve the interpretation of incoming stimuli, or the transformation of information, or the production of output.

8   The terminology here derives from the classification of writing systems. In *pictographic* systems pictorial symbols are used to represent concepts, e.g. the road signs. In a *logographic* system arbitrary symbols represent words or concepts, as in the Chinese writing system or the Japanese Kanji system. The lines and curves making up the signs do not relate in any systematic way to the sound structure of speech. The application of the term 'logographic' to English means that words are treated as though they were

logographs, i.e. without consideration of the links between the letters and their pronunciation. Harris and Coltheart (1986) provide a discussion of logographic writing systems.

9   The *phonographic* writing systems use written symbols to represent elements of speech. In a *syllabary* each symbol represents a whole syllable (as in the Japanese Kana systems). An *alphabetic* system contains symbols which represent the consonant and vowel *phonemes* of the language. In an ideal system a unified written symbol – a *grapheme* – is paired with each phoneme. This is approximated in the initial teaching alphabet. Written English is fundamentally alphabetic but departs from the ideal in various respects: (1) the number of letters used to symbolize a phoneme varies; and (2) the correspondences between graphemes and phonemes are inconsistent. Other European languages, such as Serbo-Croat, Finnish and Italian, are based on much more consistent grapheme–phoneme correspondences. These points are discussed in some of the contributions in Sterling and Robson (1992).

10  The phonological process may in part be equated with a short-term memory system which is specialized for retention of elements of speech, i.e. an articulatory component of 'working memory'. Gathercole and Baddeley (1993) have discussed the role of this system in learning to read and in other aspects of language development. The more specific reference is to the capability for division of speech into segments, often referred to as 'phonological awareness' (Goswami and Bryant, 1990).

11  Ehri (1992) equates the term 'logographic' with a pre-phonetic stage of reading development. She recognizes a semi-phonetic stage of sight word reading which involves incorporation of partial letter-sound information into an access route for a word. She would see this stage as 'alphabetic' rather than logographic. Her usage of these terms differs from the definitions which are followed in the present discussion.

12  Seymour and Elder (1986) have provided a detailed account of response patterns in logographic reading. The data were obtained from a class of children in Scotland who learned under an exclusively whole-word regime during their first school year.

13  Seymour and Evans (1992) give a detailed account of a longitudinal study in which responses to names and room words were collected.

14  Seymour and Elder (1986) presented logographic readers with familiar words printed in unfamiliar formats, for example a zigzag or vertical arrangement of letters. This manipulation could be relied on to disrupt a recognition process which depended on word shape. In fact, many of the children continued to read the words despite the distortions.

15  Seymour and Elder (1986) assessed the ability of logographic readers to discriminate between 'reading set' and other words. It was shown that the children possessed a remarkably accurate record of their reading words.

16  Letter–sound knowledge includes ability to identify the visual forms of the letters, to form them in writing, and a bi-directional link with sound.

17  This definition of alphabetic processing is restricted to 'sequential decoding' of individual letter–sound associations (Marsh et al., 1981).

18　Nonword reading (or spelling) has come to be viewed as the most effective measure of an individual's grasp of the alphabetic basis of the writing system.

19　There is some disagreement as to whether it is appropriate for children to refer to the letters by their conventional names (ay, bee, see, dee, ee, eff, jee etc.) or by a system of 'sound names' (a, buh, kuh, duh, e, fff, guh etc.). Neither system satisfactorily represents the dominant grapheme–phoneme correspondences. However, the 'sound names' appear to come closer to a reasonable representation. The vowels (a, e, i, o, u) can be given their short (checked) pronunciations and some consonants can be named in a way which minimizes the additional vowel (fff, sss, mmm, nnn, lll etc.). The remaining consonants can be pronounced with a following schwa vowel (buh, duh, kuh etc.). The children may then infer that the phonemic equivalent of the letter is the initial phoneme of its name (Stuart and Coltheart, 1988). This strategy is more difficult to apply to the conventional names of the letters. The tactic of linking letters to objects whose names start with the appropriate phoneme ('s' —> sun, sock, scissors etc.) is probably a good way of assisting the abstraction of the phonemic equivalents.

20　In the studies 'sounding' was defined in terms of visible lip movements preceding a response or audible muttering of letter sounds.

21　The letter sounding process underlying alphabetic reading may produce errors of identification or omission, transposition or addition of elements. This incorrect version of the target may match a word in the child's lexicon, resulting in a word error response. If no match is found, the incorrect version may be pronounced, resulting in a nonword error response.

22　Seymour and Evans (1992) present information about the incidence of sounding for word and nonword targets. Sequential decoding will tend to fail when words with complex or irregular structures are encountered, opening the way to the emergence of a new strategy (Marsh et al., 1981).

23　Frith (1985) proposed that alphabetic processing is established for spelling and writing before reading. This means that there may be a point in development when a child is a logographic reader but an alphabetic speller. One consequence is that children are sometimes able to write simple words which they cannot yet read (Bryant and Bradley, 1980; Seymour and Elder, 1986).

24　A syllable is defined as an obligatory vowel nucleus which may be preceded by and/or followed by a consonant or consonant group. The syllable is held to have a hierarchical structure, the first level of division being between the *onset* (initial consonant group) and the *rime* (vowel + terminal consonant group). At a second level the vowel and terminal consonant may be segregated. At the base of the hierarchy the consonant and vowel groups are unpacked as sequences of phonemes. It is suggested that the development of phonological awareness normally proceeds down this hierarchy (syllables → onsets + rimes → phonemes). Goswami and Bryant (1990) and Treiman and Zukowski (1991) provide relevant discussions.

25　Seymour and Evans (1994a) provide details of the blending and segmentation studies.

26　In the Seymour and Evans (1994a) study children gave theoretically appropriate responses to about 40 per cent of items when asked to give three segments as against about 25 per cent of items when asked to give two segments. These results were obtained at the end of the Primary 1 year. The trend was reinforced during the Primary 2 year.

27  Seymour and Evans (1992) provide details.

28  The effect of a difference in the timing of the introduction of alphabetic learning is apparent in the contrast between the studies of Seymour and Elder (1986) and Seymour and Evans (1992). The children in the first study were not taught about letters and sounds during their first year and remained logographic readers who could not attempt unfamiliar items. In the second study, alphabetic learning was introduced in the first term and the children quickly became able to tackle simple unfamiliar forms (nonwords).

29  A reasonable expectation is that the logographic and alphabetic processes might be equated with the lexical and non-lexical processes which are postulated in the dual-route model of advanced reading. However, some commentators have explicitly excluded this possibility. For example, Morton (1989) argued that the early logographic process is allowed to lapse and that it is later replaced by a 'logogen system' which is specialized for identification of morphemes.

30  In Seymour and Evans's (1992) study overt sounding tended to disappear during the second school year.

31  Seymour and Evans (1992) obtained vocal reaction time measurements for word and nonword reading from term 3 of the first school year onwards. The reaction times were classified into successive 250 ms intervals of a time range extending from 0 to 5 s and beyond. The data were plotted as frequency distributions. Results for individual cases showed a large divergence in the distributions for real words and nonwords. This was seen as consistent with the dual process account.

32  Seymour and Evans (1992) reported that in the third year at school some children began to show a convergence of the reaction time distributions. This was taken as an indication of replacement of the dual process by a single orthographic system which was capable of identifying both familiar words and unfamilar nonwords.

33  The term 'orthographic' is used in different ways. For Frith (1985) it refers to abstract letter arrays which correspond to morphemes. In the present discussion the term refers to the spelling components which provide the building blocks for representing English syllables. These are letter groups which correspond to vowels and consonant clusters or to larger structures, such as the rime. It is assumed that these structures are assembled as a 'framework' within which familiar words and legitimately structured nonwords can be represented. The computational model of Seidenberg and McClelland (1989) also postulates a single structure within which words and nonwords may be represented.

34  The value of the so-called 'whole language' approach lies in its emphasis on motivational aspects of reading. The extension of the approach to include an ideological opposition to 'phonic' methods appears less credible.

35 A teaching approach which excluded the foundations might be characterized by an absence of explicit letter-sound learning and by cafeteria access
to a wide range of texts containing a large and uncontrolled vocabulary.

36 Useful vocabularies for early logographic learning should probably include
significant numbers of interesting words of concrete (imageable) meaning.

37 There is disagreement as to whether it is worthwhile to seek to develop
'phonological awareness' in the abstract. Lundberg et al. (1988) demonstrated that ability to manipulate phonemes can be taught in a pre-school
context. However, studies with adult illiterates suggest that phonemic
awareness normally develops only in the context of learning to read an
alphabetic script (Morais, 1991).

38 Bradley and Bryant (1983) demonstrated that pre-school sensitivity to rhyme,
as indexed by ability to spot an odd-man-out in a sequence of rhyming
words, was correlated with later reading progress.

39 It is likely that the relationship between phonological awareness and reading
development is interactive. Early encounters with the alphabetic basis of
print trigger a preliminary awareness of phonemes which in turn assists the
further development of the alphabetic process. Bertelson (1987) and Goswami
and Bryant (1990) provide useful discussions.

40 Seymour (1990, 1993) has outlined an account of orthographic development
which involves a number of steps or stages. The first stage involves the
logographic and alphabetic foundation processes which have been discussed
in this chapter. It is argued that the alphabetic process provides a basis for
the formation of a 'core' orthographic structure which is defined by simple
initial consonants, short vowels and simple terminal consonants. The structure
depends on the phonological insight that a syllable has a three-dimensional
structure (initial consonant × vowel × terminal consonant). Subsequently
the 'core' structure is elaborated to include more complex consonant groups
and the principles of vowel lengthening. It is quite possible that the higher
levels of organization are based on rhyme defined word families and hence
on a two-dimensional (onset × rime) phonological structure.

41 Orthographic development can be studied using word and nonword lists
which reflect the initial consonant, vowel and terminal consonant structures
which are thought to be characteristic of the 'core' of more advanced levels.
Application of such lists to primary school children with reading ages in the
range 6–12 years suggests that the process of internalization of the complex
consonant and vowel structures continues throughout the primary school
period (Seymour, 1993).

42 The general idea here is that the initiation of reading development depends
on (i) the internalization of a sample of words containing a variety of orthographic structures (the 'logographic' process); (ii) a grasp of the dominant
letter–sound associations (the 'alphabetic' process; and (iii) a 'phonological'
process in which the hierarchical structure of the syllable is represented. The
orthographic system may then be formed by an internal process of 'rep-
resentational redescription' (Karmiloff-Smith, 1986). Frequent interaction
with print will be essential for the success of this process. This emphasizes

the importance of the motivational aspects of reading which determine the amount of experience with text.

43   The definition of reading disability and 'dyslexia' has involved much dispute. In popular terminology it is probably usual to make a distinction between an unexpected reading problem occurring in a child of normal or superior intelligence ('dyslexia') and the general run of 'garden variety' reading difficulties which may be encountered in children of lower intelligence. However, there is no real agreement as to how the line between these categories might be drawn (Stanovich, 1991).

44   There is evidence to support a genetic and neurobiological basis of dyslexia. These aspects are considered in papers contained in Galaburda (1989) and Snowling and Thomson (1991).

45   An assessment of foundation level processes can easily be carried out using (i) lists of high frequency words which are commonly found in the early stages of reading schemes and which cannot easily be read by letter–sound translation ('logographic' process); (ii) sounding of letters and writing letters in response to their sounds; (iii) reading and writing simple Consonant – Vowel – Consonant nonwords ('alphabetic' process), A primary logographic impairment is suggested if the child appears unable to read words directly and if large efforts in teaching are needed to expand the vocabulary. A primary alphabetic impairment is suggested if the nonwords cause extreme difficulty and if large teaching efforts are needed to establish the basis of letter–sound reading.

46   It is sometimes argued that remedial teaching should focus on the 'strengths'. At the foundation level it seems desirable to emphasize both the logographic and the alphabetic aspect and to make particular efforts to establish the weaker process.

47   A 'cognitive assessment method' designed to investigate more advanced levels of reading disability has been established. This is based on the contrast between real words and nonwords and uses information from reaction times and errors to infer the underlying character of an individual's reading and spelling processes. Application of the method suggests that there are individual variations in the nature of the dysfunction underlying the reading disability. Details are provided by Seymour (1986) for adolescent cases and by Seymour and Evans (1993, 1994b) for primary school cases.

48   Cognitive research into reading acquisition and reading disability in the classroom requires the permission and co-operation of parents, class teachers, head teachers and, in many instances, officials employed by local educational authorities.

## REFERENCES

Bertelson, P. 1987: *The Onset of Literacy*, Cambridge, MA: MIT Press.

Bradley, L. and Bryant, P.E. 1983: 'Categorising sounds and learning to read: a causal connection', *Nature*, 301, 419–21.

Bryant, P.E. and Bradley, L. 1980: 'Why children sometimes write words which they do not read', in U. Frith (ed.), *Cognitive Processes in Spelling*, London: Academic Press.

Ehri, L. 1992: 'Reconceptualising the development of sight word reading and its relationship to recoding', in P. Gough, L. Ehri and R. Treiman (eds), *Literacy Acquisition*, Hillsdale, NJ: Lawrence Erlbaum Associates.

Ellis, A.W. 1984: *Reading, Writing and Dyslexia*, Hove: Lawrence Erlbaum Associates.

Frith, U. 1985: 'Beneath the surface of developmental dyslexia', in K.E. Patterson, J.C. Marshall and M. Coltheart (eds), *Surface Dyslexia: Neuropsychological and Cognitive Studies of Phonological Reading*, Hove: Lawrence Erlbaum Associates.

Galaburda, A.M. 1989: *From Reading to Neurons*, Cambridge, MA: MIT Press.

Gathercole, S.E. and Baddeley, A.D. 1993: *Working Memory and Language*, Hove: Lawrence Erlbaum Associates.

Goswami, U. and Bryant, P.E. 1990: *Phonological Skills and Learning to Read.* Hove: Lawrence Erlbaum Associates.

Gough, P.B. and Hillinger, M.L. 1980: 'Learning to read: an unnatural act', *Bulletin of the Orton Society*, 30, 179–95.

Harris, M. and Coltheart, M. 1986: *Language Processing in Children and Adults*, London: Routledge and Kegan Paul.

Karmiloff-Smith, A. 1986: 'From metaprocesses to conscious access: evidence from children's metalinguistic and repair data', *Cognition*, 23, 95–147.

Lundberg, I., Frost, J. and Petersen, O. 1988: 'Effects of an extensive programme for stimulating phonological awareness in pre-school children', *Reading Research Quarterly*, 23, 262–84.

Marsh, G., Friedman, M., Welch, V. and Desberg, P. 1981: 'A cognitive-developmental theory of reading acquisition', in G.E. MacKinnon and T.G. Waller (eds), *Reading Research: Advances in Theory and Practice*, vol. 3, New York: Academic Press.

Morais, J. 1991: 'Constraints on the development of phonemic awareness', in S.A. Brady and D.P. Shankweiler (eds), *Phonological Processes in Literacy*, Hillsdale, NJ: Lawrence Erlbaum Associates.

Morton, J. 1989: 'An information-processing account of reading acquisition', in A. Galaburda (ed.), *From Reading to Neurons*, Cambridge, MA: MIT Press.

Seidenberg, M.S. and McClelland, J.L. 1989: 'A distributed, developmental model of word recognition and naming', *Psychological Review*, 96, 522–68.

Seymour, P.H.K. 1986: *Cognitive Analysis of Dyslexia*, London: Routledge and Kegan Paul.

—— 1990: 'Developmental dyslexia', in M.W. Eysenck (ed.), *Cognitive Psychology: An International Review*, Chichester: Wiley.

—— 1993: 'Un modèle du développement orthographique à double fondation', in J.-P. Jaffre, L. Sprenger-Charolles and M. Fayol (eds), *Lecture-écriture Acquisition: Les Actes de la VillettePI*, Paris: Nathan Pedagogie.

—— and Elder, L. 1986: 'Beginning reading without phonology', *Cognitive Neuropsychology*, 3, 1–36.

—— and Evans, H.M. 1992: 'Beginning reading without semantics: a cognitive study of hyperlexia', *Cognitive Neuropsychology*, 9, 89–122.

—— and —— 1993: 'The visual (orthographic) processor and developmental dyslexia', in D. Willows, R. Kruk and E. Corcos (eds), *Visual Processes in Reading and Reading Disabilities*, Hillsdale, NJ: Lawrence Erlbaum Associates.

—— and —— 1994a: 'Levels of phonological awareness and learning to read', *Reading and Writing: An Interdisciplinary Journal*, 6, 221–50.

—— and —— 1994b: 'Sources of constraint and individual variations in normal and impaired spelling', in G.D.A. Brown and N.C. Ellis (eds), *Handbook of Spelling: Theory, Process and Intervention*, Chichester: Wiley.

Snowling, M.J. and Thomson, M. 1991: *Dyslexia: Integrating Theory and Practice*, London: Whurr.

Stanovich, K.E. 1991: 'The theoretical and practical consequences of discrepancy definitions of dyslexia', in M. Snowling and M. Thomson (eds), *Dyslexia: Integrating Theory and Practice*, London: Whurr.

Sterling, C.M. and Robson, C. 1992: *Psychology, Spelling and Education,* Clevedon: Multilingual Matters.

Stuart, M. and Coltheart, M. 1988: 'Does reading develop in a sequence of stages?' *Cognition*, 30, 139–81.

Treiman, R. and Zukowski, A. 1991: 'Levels of phonological awareness', in S.A. Brady and D.P. Shankweiler (eds), *Phonological Processes in Literacy*, Hillsdale, NJ: Lawrence Erlbaum Associates.

# 4

## *Assessing Reading Skills*
### Nata Goulandris and Margaret Snowling

At the close of the previous chapter, Philip Seymour and Henryka Evans suggest that children who lag behind in reading have probably failed to develop the fundamental processes required for reading. This chapter takes up this issue.

Although a classroom may contain as many as forty children, the teacher has to be concerned with the successes and failures of individual children, rather than the class as a whole. This means that when a child fails, it is necessary to understand why. While the results of standardized tests of reading will show that a child is failing relative to most children of the same chronological age, the result will not indicate where the problems lie. Knowing the reading age of a child is only a beginning; the investigation into the particular difficulties begins rather than finishes there.

Assessment of the linguistic difficulties of children who fail to read normally is still developing; nevertheless, a significant advance has been made in the tools that can be used to investigate the nature and extent of the reading processes available to individual children.

The most important clues can be found in the words of the language itself, for written words differ in the degree to which they tap particular reading processes. Irregular words, such as have, was, pint, bear, require the use of lexical processes if they are to be pronounced correctly; while regular words such as those, but, face, may be read by either lexical or sublexical means; and nonwords require the use of sublexical procedures.

*Using a selection of different types of written material, Nata Goulandris and Margaret Snowling show how these can be used to reveal the deficient reading processes in individual children. The mistakes that children make in these tests provide additional clues to the problem.*

*Since theory is often simpler than practice, the authors report a number of investigations of individual children using the techniques discussed in the chapter. The children vary, some having specific difficulties with phonological skills, others with word recognition. Most, however, have some difficulties in more than one domain.*

*Because this work is relatively new and still developing, there are as yet no tests available with norms for each age group. Nevertheless, it should be possible for teachers in the classroom to apply the approach outlined here to individual children across a range of ages, drawing from the reading vocabulary appropriate to the child's reading stage and recording and analysing the mistakes the child makes. The importance of this chapter is that it begins to show the way.*

There is nothing more disheartening for a teacher than to face the fact that one child or even a number of children in a class are not reading adequately. Of course reading difficulties can be the consequence of many factors, some cognitive, some affective, and it is never easy to pinpoint the causes. In this chapter we will focus exclusively on the reading process itself, considering ways of analysing children's current reading strategies in order to construct an individualized teaching programme which will address a child's problems with reading at a specific point in time. The aim is to investigate the range of reading strategies that a child has available in order to help him or her develop a more flexible and effective approach. We believe that it is also necessary to assess spelling and underlying phonological skills to obtain a comprehensive picture of a child's current skills.

There are three distinctive reading skills which contribute to competent reading: the ability to recognize familiar written words; the ability to use phonic skills to pronounce unfamiliar words and the ability to understand what is being read (these skills are discussed further in chapter 2). Good readers can shift between alternative strategies, as needed, so that reading progresses as efficiently as possible.[1] However, some individuals may be unable to acquire one or more of these component skills and may consequently lag behind classmates.

During development, the three skills are, to a considerable degree, independent of each other. A reader may rely primarily on one skill and rarely make use of the others. For example, a child may have excellent comprehension, moderate word recognition ability and poor phonic recoding skills. This profile is characteristic of many children with developmental dyslexia whose difficulties with recognizing and identifying speech sounds prevent them from perceiving the relationship between letters and the sounds each letter usually represents. Maggie Snowling has demonstrated that developmental dyslexics have poor recoding skills but often learn to compensate by using their more proficient reading strategies.[2] Another type of reader, the hyperlexic, has excellent phonic recoding ability, and good recognition skills but is quite unable to understand the words which are pronounced so proficiently.[3] Most readers' strengths and weaknesses lie somewhere between these extremes.

Degree of competence is also an important consideration. Obviously beginners have fewer strategies at their disposal and are less skilled than more experienced readers. In normal development, the strategies readers use will change with time as reading skill progresses and alternative strategies become available. However, children with reading difficulties are often unable to acquire alternative strategies or may have become overly dependent on one particular type of reading strategy.[4,5]

It is only when a teacher is able to understand the unique combination of strengths and weaknesses which contribute to each child's reading profile that it is possible to devise suitable individualized remedial programmes. Of course, these assessments are lengthy and time consuming and cannot be undertaken if time has not been specifically allocated for the task. Moreover, assessment of reading difficulties should not be considered a once only phenomenon but needs to be an ongoing process so that emerging strengths and current problems can be identified and evaluated. How else can we judge how much a child has progressed and whether the child's strategies are improving?

## The Importance of Lexical Word Recognition

In reading, word recognition occurs when a written word is recognized as a familiar word and pronounced correctly, regardless of whether it appears in isolation or embedded in text. Skilled readers recognize familiar written words automatically, using direct visual word recognition. The automaticity of this process is particularly striking when a reader has been asked *not* to read a word as in an experiment originated by Stroop[6] in which subjects are asked to name the colour of the ink used to print a word. If the words are nonsense words (e.g. 'slint' or 'prundlet'), it is simple to name the colour of ink used because the nonsense words are unfamiliar and are not immediately recognized. However, if the words are names of colours printed in a different colour the task becomes quite a challenge. Faced with the word 'green' printed in red, it becomes extremely difficult to inhibit one's automatic reading response in order to identify the colour of the ink. So we shout out 'green' before we can respond correctly. An experiment such as this enables us to experience the tremendous speed and automaticity of word recognition. We are so used to recognizing words instantly and without effort that there is inclination to overlook the importance of this process.

In addition, there has been a tendency for word recognition to be dismissed by some researchers as if it was of no consequence. For example, Kenneth Goodman[7] and Frank Smith[8] have suggested that readers identify words primarily through context, using psycholinguistic cues to assist them. Smith argues that the readers' prior knowledge of language structure and ability to predict which words are likely to appear next, enables readers to identify words without having to pay more than cursory attention to them. This view has been strongly contested by Keith Stanovich[9] who has countered that good readers identify words as wholes and do not rely on context for word recognition. It is the struggling poor readers who require, and often profit substantially from, the assistance of context.

Moreover, many teachers have been led to believe that reading words out of context is an unnecessary skill and that word recognition is of no consequence. This view is both misleading and inaccurate. Word recognition or lexical processing is a vitally important component of skilled reading and the inability to learn to recognize written words accurately and automatically needs to be evaluated and the specific problems documented (see chapter 2 for further discussion of lexical processes). Therefore, when assessing reading it is important to examine an individual's ability to read both text and single words presented out of context so that linguistic and contextual cues are no longer available to assist word recognition.

## Assessing word recognition – single word reading

Standardized reading tests provide an indication of how an individual performs in relation to the rest of his peers and is a useful first step in confirming or allaying a teacher's concern. Single word reading can be initially assessed using a single word standardized reading test such as the Macmillan[10] or the Schonell Graded Reading Test.[11] Both these tests consist of a list of words graded in order of difficulty. Testing is discontinued when the reader has made more than the prescribed number of errors. A reading age or a standard score can then be calculated, enabling teachers to compare the performance of the child tested with that of children of the same chronological age. Of course, reading standards vary between schools and between different areas. However, if a child's reading age is eighteen months or more below the child's chronological age, further assessment should be undertaken. In the case of children below the age of 8, a twelve-month discrepancy between reading performance and chronological age may indicate potential reading difficulties. It should be noted that, for children of a given age, reading ages may vary widely. It is therefore essential to judge a child's performance in relation to the rest of the class. It is also important to keep in mind that some particularly able children may be under-achieving even though their reading age corresponds to their chronological age.

A reading age score in itself provides little useful information apart from signalling the existence of a potential or current problem. It is therefore essential to keep detailed notes of errors made and how the reader attempts to process the words, differentiating between words which are recognized immediately using lexical processing and words which are sounded out audibly or subvocally using sublexical processing (see chapter 2 for further discussion of sublexical processing). Once errors have been recorded it is possible to examine them and attempt to understand why the child is making these errors.

Error analysis should then be performed to evaluate the quality of the child's response and the type of strategy used. Of particular concern is whether the reader is able to recognize whole words accurately and whether word recognition is reliable and consistent or is based on imprecise visual cues leading to numerous inaccurate guesses. In addition, it is important to investigate which strategies a reader adopts when reading unfamiliar words.

## Regularity

Written words can be categorized as regular or irregular according to the predictability of their spelling. Some words can be sounded out and spelled just as they sound. Such words are often referred to as regular words since their pronunciations conform to the most common mappings between letters and sounds, for example 'ham', 'piglet', 'carpenter'. In contrast, irregular words incorporate unusual spellings which learners are unlikely to recognize unless they have previously encountered the item and linked it to the word's meaning and correct pronunciation. In order to read an irregular word correctly a reader has to be familiar with the word and has to have formed a word recognition unit for its unusual spelling. Regular words can be read using either the lexical route (whole word recognition) or the sublexical route (recoding) whereas irregular words can only be read using a lexical route. We can therefore use regular words to examine a child's ability to make use of alphabetic information and irregular words to assess word recognition (for discussion of lexical and sublexical processes, see chapters 2 and 3).

As beginners are initially unaware of letter–sound mappings they find both regular and irregular words equally difficult. Once they begin to understand the nature of letter–sound correspondences, they tend to find regular words substantially easier than irregular words. In contrast, at this stage, they often misread irregular words, using phonological strategies to recode them and pronouncing them as if they were regular words, for example 'island' read as 'izland', 'sign' read with the silent letter 'g' sounded, 'flood' read as if it rhymes with 'food', 'pint' read as 'pinnt', 'sword' read with the 'w' sounded and 'colonel' pronounced as 'collonnel'. Such errors are usually referred to as regularizations because irregular words are inappropriately treated as if they were regular. Regularization errors indicate that the reader is unable to recognize a word lexically and is attempting to use sublexical phonic recoding processes in order to identify it. Very occasionally children misinterpret the reading task thinking that sublexical processing is a mandatory part of reading and consequently become overdependent on phonic recoding. Generally, however, readers who make numerous regularizations when compared with readers of the same reading age have difficulty establishing a functional visual recognition system. (Regular and irregular words will be discussed further below.)

In order to compare children's ability to read regular and irregular words one needs to use a test which has been properly designed so that each pair of regular and irregular words has been matched according to number of letters, number of syllables, frequency of occurrence in written text and part of speech. To use the test presented here (table 4.1), teachers will need to write each word on a separate index card. For the purposes of scoring, regular words may be written in one colour and irregular words in another colour. Cards should be shuffled so that the words are presented in random order. Teachers will also need a copy of the list to use as a marking sheet when hearing the child read the words. All incorrect responses should be recorded in detail for subsequent error analysis.

For the assessment of word recognition, teachers will be primarily interested in the reader's ability to read irregular words. This should be followed by an error analysis along the lines described below. (The reader may consult the word recognition error analysis questions reported below for guidance.) Error analysis will enable teachers to have a much clearer picture of the strategies currently used by the reader to identify irregular words.

*Table 4.1*   Regularity

Print these words individually on cards and present them in random order.
Record all reading responses.

| Regular | | Irregular | |
| --- | --- | --- | --- |
| *One syllable* | *Two syllable* | *One syllable* | *Two syllable* |
| siege | bitter | choir | double |
| grill | thimble | flood | sausage |
| drug | tutor | aunt | loser |
| slot | lobster | wolf | lettuce |
| lime | market | pint | police |
| film | divine | sign | steady |
| task | organ | dove | lever |
| shin | lemon | wand | litre |
| hatch | trumpet | bread | island |
| spade | mixture | glove | colonel |
| prince | rubber | tongue | marine |
| plug | tumble | bowl | biscuit |
| blade | | swan | |
| bleat | | shove | |
| snail | | suede | |
| globe | | sword | |
| cask | | vase | |
| match | | breath | |
| sand | | ward | |

**Control data**
Number of words read correctly (maximum, 31)

| *Reading age* | | *Regular* | *Irregular* |
| --- | --- | --- | --- |
| 7 years | Mean | 17.25 | 9.75 |
| | SD | 5.6 | 5.2 |
| | Range | 9–28 | 3–22 |

A score below 7 on regular words and 3 on irregular words falls below the
norm

| 10 years | Mean | 29.6 | 26.0 |
| --- | --- | --- | --- |
| | SD | 1.7 | 2.5 |
| | Range | 25–31 | 22–30 |

A score below 26 on regular words and 21 on irregular words falls below
the norm

*Source*: Snowling, M.J., Stackhouse, J. and Rack, J.P. (1986) 'Phonological dyslexia
and dysgraphia: a developmental analysis', *Cognitive Neuropsychology*, 3, 309–39

## Error analysis

Readers' errors provide valuable clues about the types of strategies adopted. For example, if a child reads 'organ' as 'orange', mistakenly identifying the target word as a visually similar real word, the error indicates that word recognition strategies were used. In contrast, when a reader identifies an inconsistent word such as 'head' as 'heed' or tries to sound out words aloud but does not manage to arrive at the correct pronunciation, this can be considered as an indication that sublexical processing was attempted. Errors may be classified as follows: visually similar, regularizations, unsuccessful sound attempts and refusals.

## Visually similar real word errors

When a target word is misread as another word which resembles it, because they both contain some of the same letters, i.e. 'money' read as 'morning', 'rubber' read as 'rabbit' or 'litre' read as 'little', the response can be classified as a visually similar word error. Such errors indicate that the child is using visual 'look and say' strategies or lexical word recognition. In early reading the resemblance between the word read and the response are approximate.[12] Usually only a few of the letters contained in the target word are present in the response, generally the initial letter; for example 'puppy' read as 'people', 'as' read as 'at', 'horse' read as 'has'. There is a greater overlap between the word the child is attempting to read and the response given in the visual errors of more advanced readers, i.e. 'house' read as 'horse', 'choir' read as 'chair' or as 'chore'. The degree of visual overlap between the target and the response can therefore serve as a useful measure of the amount of letter information to which the child is paying attention[12] (see also chapter 2).

## Unsuccessful sound attempts

Unsuccessful sound attempts occur when the reader tries to sound out a word but cannot execute the process correctly. Failure may occur at one or more of three different levels:

1   parsing – the reader is unable to separate the letters in the
    word appropriately before applying sound–letter rules ('then'
    read as /t/ /h/ /e/ /n/ with the first two letters considered as
    separate speech sounds);
2   incomplete knowledge of letter–sound rules;
3   blending skills are poor.

It is necessary to sort unsuccessful sound attempts errors into
these categories in order to pinpoint the exact areas(s) of difficulty.

## Regularization errors

Regularization errors occur when an irregular word is pronounced
as if it were a regular word (i.e. 'flood' read as if it rhymes with
'food', 'pint' read as 'pinnt') and have already been discussed more
extensively above. Regularization errors show that the reader is
successfully applying recoding skills on words which require word-
specific knowledge.

## Refusals

A response is classified as a refusal when a reader is unable to
respond. Refusals are generally produced by children who have
no phonic skills at their disposal to help them recode an unfamiliar
word. In the early stages of reading, this is a common response
because many beginning readers rely primarily on visual word recognition supported by picture and semantic cues. When unfamiliar words are encountered out of context, beginners are unable to
identify them. As reading skill improves and the ability to understand sound–letter mappings develops, the incidence of refusals
tends to decrease substantially and learners are able to use knowledge of letter–sound correspondences when attempting to read
unfamiliar words. Refusals are by no means always a mark of complete ignorance. For some children their occurrence shows a distinct
step forward, replacing a stage of arbitrary guessing and showing

that the reader now recognizes that each individual word is associated with a meaning and that arbitrary guessing is inappropriate.

## Other errors

Invariably some errors will not fall neatly into these categories. For example, 'shin' read as 'shine' poses a problem because it is difficult to determine why the child has misread the word. Has the child simply used a letter-name strategy when reading the vowel or does this error indicate a general tendency to confuse visually similar words. Such errors require further investigation and attempts should be made to identify similar errors on other occasions and try to detect the origin of this type of error. For example, if 'win' is read as 'wine' and 'bit' as 'bite', it is likely that the reader is using a letter name strategy when recoding the vowel. In this case teaching the child about the function of the silent 'e' would help the child to understand that vowels have more than one sound, that all vowels have a short and a long sound and that the long sound is the same as the name of the letter. In English, the spelling of the long vowel is usually (but not always) represented by an additional letter such as the 'e' in words such as 'fine', 'site', 'lane' and 'mope'.

Error analysis should address the following questions;

1 Is word recognition developing normally? Are words which should be familiar identified correctly?
2 Is rate of word identification fast, average, slow, very slow?
3 Is there a predominance of visually similar real word errors, indicating that the reader is identifying words using partial cues?
4 What is the degree of visual overlap between target and response?
5 Is there a predominance of sounding out errors suggesting:
   (a)  excessive reliance on phonic recoding?
   (b)  unreliable phonic recoding skills?
   (c)  weak blending skills?
6 Is there a predominance of refusals suggesting that the child has limited sight vocabulary and immature word attack skills?

## Assessing single word reading skills: two case studies

Max's single word reading was typical of many poor readers. He was 10 years 6 months at the time of this assessment. On the British Ability Scales (BAS) Test of Word Reading[13] he attained a reading age of 7 years 5 months, three years below his chronological age. He made many visually similar real word errors. For example, he read 'glove' as 'glory', 'men' as 'man', 'dig' as 'big', 'lawn' as 'learn', 'guest' as 'gust', 'ladies' as 'lady' and 'collect' as 'call'. All these errors indicated that Max often used partial lexical information when identifying words, even particularly easy ones such as 'dig' and 'men'. One of his errors suggested that he could use phonic recoding when absolutely necessary. He sounded out 'drab' extremely slowly and painstakingly, managing to blend the sounds correctly, but he used this procedure only once. At this stage in his reading development, Max was relying almost exclusively on approximate visual recognition. The consequence of this immature strategy is that he misread many words when they were presented out of context and had a poorly developed word recognition system.

However, when Max was asked to read the thirty-one regular and thirty-one irregular words presented above, he did surprisingly well on the regular words, displaying an ability to use phonic recoding skills. He read twenty-six regular words such as 'thimble', 'lemon' and 'trumpet' but only eleven of the irregular words correctly. What was interesting was that he was much less reliant on visual strategies in this test than he was when tested on the standardized test. Although he made several immature visually based errors – 'colonel' read as 'cola', 'suede' read as 'sunny', 'biscuit' read as 'dust' – the majority of his errors demonstrated that he was attempting to use phonics, i.e. 'wand' read to rhyme with 'sand', 'loser' read as 'loaser' and 'lettuce' read as 'letyoos'. Like many poor readers he had a wider range of reading strategies than he tended to use spontaneously.

Harry was 8 years 6 months old when he was first seen. He attained a reading age of 6 years 3 months on the BAS Test of Word Reading which placed him at the third centile, indicating a very poor standard for his age. He managed to read only a few of the words on the BAS, although the test contains many common high frequency words such as 'the', 'you' and 'he' which beginning readers often encounter in their early books. Not surprisingly, he was also completely unable to read any of the regular and irregular words in the more difficult test of regularity. He guessed his way through both lists, making visually based errors which relied almost exclusively on first letter cues, i.e. 'wood' read as 'when' and 'where', 'ring' as 'run', 'slot' as 'so', 'bleat' as 'butter', 'flood' as 'forest', 'globe' as 'getting', 'marine' as 'mum' (see chapter 2 for discussion of letter cues in reading). Occasionally his errors took account of more than first letter information but deviated substantially from the correct response, i.e. 'choir' read as 'chip'. Some errors retained both initial and final letters, i.e. 'ship' read as 'shop', 'sand' read as 'said', 'bowl' read as 'ball' and 'dig' read as 'dog'. About 10 per cent of his errors were more difficult to interpret, i.e. 'match' read as 'humming', 'drug' as 'grog', 'bitter' as 'tub', 'mixture' as 'next', 'biscuit' as 'tan'. In the case of 'drug', 'match' and 'biscuit' he chose responses which began with the words' final letters. In the case of the word 'mixture', both the target and his response 'next' shared the letters 'xt'. Thus he sometimes appeared to be identifying a letter or a group of letters in the target word, regardless of their position within the word, and arbitrarily selecting a response which either began with or contained the letter(s).

He also made a few unsuccessful sound attempts. For 'plug' he managed to sound out each of the letters but failed to blend them correctly, eventually identifying the word as 'pun'. He used a similar procedure for 'lemon' which was read as 'lawn'. Since Harry had no problems finding the correct sound for each of the letters in these words, his errors suggest that his primary difficulty with recoding was recalling the sequence of sounds in order to blend them correctly and then finding the word which appropriately matched the speech sounds he had produced. Harry's word recognition was not only extremely poor but lacked direction. He had some vague notions about using first letter cues but was unable to follow that principle in 10 per cent of his attempts. He also had some rudimentary understanding of letter–sound rules but was as yet unable to apply them effectively.

## The importance of the phonological component

When required to read unfamiliar words out of context, most readers will attempt to use sublexical processing, applying their knowledge of letter–sound relationships to recode the words. The shortcomings of the phonics approach is widely recognized. As many English words are irregular, they cannot be correctly identified unless the reader has lexical knowledge linking the word's spelling to its meaning and pronunciation. Moreover, many more words contain inconsistent spelling patterns, rendering the identification of the words through phonic recoding problematic, for example the 'ea' in 'head' can be pronounced like the 'ee' in 'bee' or like the 'e' in 'bed'. Despite these severe limitations, learning to recode accurately and quickly provides the learner with the requisite tools needed to read independently without constant help. Not only can the emergent recoder begin to decipher words which he could not previously identify, but he can eventually construct the pronunciations of totally new words which he has never heard before, making reading a valuable source of information about new vocabulary. Once this level of proficiency has been achieved, reading is no longer highly dependent on a child's existing language skills but can now begin to extend existing linguistic knowledge.

Understanding sound–letter mapping procedures is therefore an essential step in the smooth and efficient acquisition of reading skills.[12] The primary role of phonics is to enable the beginner to 'crack the code', i.e. to understand that spellings are by no means arbitrary but that the underlying system of sound-to-spelling mappings provides essential information about how a word on the page might be pronounced. In time, an appreciation of these alphabetic regularities enables children to construct a systematic representation of how the spelling of a word and its pronunciation are related to each other. Such understanding permits prediction, making orthography more meaningful, and allows the gradual, often unconscious understanding of underlying orthographic regularities. Second, phonic recoding is the key to deciphering unfamiliar words, giving learners a high degree of independence. Despite the recognized limitations of phonic strategies when recoding words which are not completely regular, in practice many children are able to apply phonic skills successfully even when

identifying irregular words. Although the clues derived are incomplete, they often provide enough information to enable the
reader to make an informed guess as to the identity of the word,
particularly when contextual support is available. In contrast, readers with poor phonic skills have difficulty reading words which
they have never encountered before and whose meaning is not
evident through context. Consequently they are always dependent on others to provide the correct pronunciation.

The ability to read and spell has proved to be highly dependent
on the learner's underlying phonological skills.[14,15] Learners who
have well-developed rhyming skills, who are able to categorize
words according to their initial, middle and final sounds, who can
manipulate speech sounds adding and subtracting them with ease,
will find it easier to recognize that letters in written words represent speech sounds than learners who have no awareness of speech
sounds. Thus phonological awareness, awareness of speech sounds,
is a powerful predictor of eventual success in the acquisition of
reading skills[14] and lack of awareness of speech sounds should
alert teachers to potential reading and spelling difficulties.[2] There
is also considerable evidence to show that children who have difficulties with phonological skills are seriously handicapped during
their reading development. The best documented case is J.M., a
developmental dyslexic described by Snowling and colleagues.[4]
J.M. had severe and resilient problems with nonword reading and
his word recognition skills developed at only half the average
rate.[16] He also remained a very poor speller over some six years
in which his progress was followed.

## Assessing sublexical recoding

When listening to a child whose reading of single words consists
of wild guesses it is often painfully obvious that the reader is
completely unable to use sound–letter information to guide their
reading attempts. What are the best ways of assessing recoding
skills? Although it is, of course, possible simply to note how a
child reads a list of regular words it is often difficult to determine
whether the reader is using word recognition or recoding skills
when reading the words. More precise ways of assessing recoding

are needed. Tests such as nonword reading and a comparison of regular and irregular words are more informative measures of recoding ability.

## Nonword reading

Nonwords are meaningless letter strings which usually resemble English words and conform to the spelling structure of English. Often these nonsense words are constructed by altering only one letter of a real word, i.e. 'house' can be changed to 'vouse' or 'fouse' and 'soldier' to 'koldier'. Nonword reading tests enable us to obtain a more accurate measure of a reader's phonic recoding ability because nonwords can only be read using the sublexical route. When nonwords are also analogues of real irregular words (i.e. 'dolonel' or 'fiscuit'), it is possible to observe whether a reader notices the relationship and readily makes use of lexical information or whether a sound–letter recoding strategy is used. Reading nonsense words or nonwords is an invaluable instrument in the test batteries of cognitive psychologists because the task clearly differentiates children who can recode easily and those who cannot. (See Rack et al. for a review of nonword reading in dyslexia.)[17]

We have found the following nonword reading test in table 4.2 useful in our assessments. The nonwords should be printed individually on index cards. Begin by presenting the ten one-syllable words in random order, followed by the remaining two-syllable words also in random order. The following instructions should be given before presenting the test.

> I am going to ask you to read some make-believe words. These make-believe words sound like words but they do not make sense. Even though they don't make sense it is possible to read them. See how many of them you can read.

If the reader finds the task very difficult, discontinue it after the first ten one-syllable items. Many readers have no problems reading the simpler one-syllable words but find the two-syllable nonwords extremely troublesome.

It is important to record all responses as faithfully as possible so

*Table 4.2* Nonword reading test

Have the child read the following nonwords. Each nonword should be written on a separate card. Record reading responses in detail.

Either a regular or an irregular pronunciation is acceptable, i.e. if 'jint' is read as rhyming with 'lint' it is regular whereas if 'jint' is read as rhyming with 'pint' it is irregular; 'soser' read as 'soaser' is regular, rhyming with 'loser' is irregular.

| One syllable | Two syllable |
|---|---|
| plood | louble |
| aund | hausage |
| wolt | soser |
| jint | pettuce |
| hign | kolice |
| pove | skeady |
| wamp | dever |
| cread | bitre |
| slove | islank |
| fongue | polonel |
| nowl | narine |
| swad | kiscuit |
| chove | |
| duede | |
| sworf | |
| jase | |
| freath | |
| warg | |
| choiy | |

**Control data**
Nonwords read correctly

| Reading age | | One syllable | Two syllable |
|---|---|---|---|
| 7 years | Mean | 9.5 | 3.6 |
| | SD | 3.6 | 2.9 |
| | Range | 3–16 | 0–9 |

A score below 3 on one-syllable words falls significantly below the norm

| 10 years | Mean | 17.3 | 10.7 |
|---|---|---|---|
| | SD | 1.4 | 1.8 |
| | Range | 15–16 | 6–12 |

A score below 14 on one-syllable and 7 on two-syllable words falls significantly below the norm

*Source*: Snowling, M.J., Stackhouse, J. and Rack, J.P. (1986) 'Phonological dyslexia and dysgraphia: a developmental analysis', *Cognitive Neuropsychology*, 3, 309–39

that detailed analysis can be completed later. Pronunciations arrived at either through the use of sound–letter rules or through lexical analogy with an irregular word are correct. For example 'plood' can be read as if it rhymed with 'food' or with 'good' and 'kolice' read as 'koalice' (regular) or by analogy to 'police' (irregular).

It is essential to identify the precise nature of each individual's recoding problem. Readers who have poor sublexical processing skills may have difficulties with one or more of the three component procedures: parsing, sound–letter knowledge and blending. Although, when recoding, one letter usually corresponds to one speech sound or phoneme, sometimes one phoneme is represented by a grapheme consisting of two letters, i.e. 'th' in the word 'thin', 'sh' in 'ship', 'ch' in 'chin' or 'gh' in 'cough'. Parsing is the procedure used to decide how many letters will correspond to a single phoneme. The reader who sounds out the word 'shelf' as /s/ /h/ /e/ /l/ /f/ is parsing incorrectly and needs to be taught that recoding cannot always be performed letter by letter.

It is also necessary to check the letter-name and letter-sound knowledge of children who are unable to recode nonwords. Usually these children have been unable to extrapolate letter–sound rules from their reading and teachers will need to identify the precise gaps and provide appropriate instruction. Often basic sound–letter relationships are reasonably secure, but knowledge of digraphs ('sh', 'ch', 'th' etc.), short vowels (the sound of 'i' in 'pin' and the 'u' in 'plum'), consonant blends ('bl', 'pr', 'sw', 'squ', 'spr' etc.) or vowel digraphs ('oa','ow', 'ee', 'ea', 'au', 'aw', 'ew' etc.) may be poor. Inability to blend can be easily evaluated during the nonword reading test and difficulties at that level should be clearly differentiated from problems which may occur at the level of parsing or rule knowledge.

Error analysis will once again provide information about the strategies the reader is adopting. A letter-by-letter strategy is evident when each letter is sounded out in turn and the sounds blended to form a word (/p/ /e/ /n/ → 'pen'). It can be contrasted with the more advanced 'chunking' approach in which readers recode larger units as wholes.[12] For example, syllables such as 'car', 'pen', 'ter', common letter strings, for example 'ing', 'tion', 'ture', or morphemes such as the 'auto' segment in 'automobile' may all be processed in their entirety rather than letter by letter.

An alternative strategy, the analogy strategy, is adopted when the reader realizes that the spelling of the new word resembles a familiar word and reads the nonwords by analogy to the known one, altering only the divergent portion.[18] Using this strategy the reader retains a large proportion of the lexical information of the analogous word such as its pronunciation and the location of the stressed syllable.

## Regularity effect

Once readers have started to learn basic letter–sound mapping procedures, they begin to show a regularity effect, finding regular words easier to read than irregular words. This regularity effect, which indicates increasing familiarity with letter–sound correspondences and a growing ability to predict correct pronunciations, can occur even though the child may never use recoding when faced with an unfamiliar word. Readers who rely exclusively on visual recognition may not be subject to this regularity effect. Teachers can compare a reader's performance on regular and irregular words to see whether readers can make use of phonic regularity. The effects of regularity change as a function of reading experience. Regular high frequency words are initially easier to read than irregular high frequency words. As reader's experience of text increases, regular words lose their advantage. However, even skilled readers demonstrate regularity effects when reading words which occur infrequently and may not have been encountered before. The test of regularity presented earlier includes norms for children whose reading age was 8 or 10 years. Examination of these norms shows that, on this test, the reading age 8 readers find regular words substantially easier than irregular words but this no longer occurs at reading age 10, when readers are able to read almost all the items in both lists.

On the nonword reading test, Max (whose reading of words was reported above) read nine in ten of the simple nonwords (i.e. 'tig', 'pab') and fourteen in twenty-two of the more difficult nonwords (i.e. 'smade' and 'baltrid'). He read the more demanding list extremely slowly suggesting that phonic recoding was still an artificial strategy for him and was not likely to occur spontaneously when he was reading on his own. Nevertheless, his attempts rarely digressed more than one or two phonemes from the target, i.e. 'tegwop' read as 'tegwoop', 'rasgan' read as 'rasan'. It was therefore possible to conclude that the prolonged teaching he had received over a number of years had resulted in moderate phonic recoding ability enabling him to make reasonable recoding attempts when tackling simple unfamiliar words. Longer words were still likely to present insurmountable problems. He now needed to be taught to divide polysyllabic words into syllables, sounding out one syllable at a time and then blending the result.

Harry (whose word reading we reported above) managed to read only two in ten of the simple nonwords correctly, 'hiv' and 'tig'. Although he was unable to read the others, he nevertheless attempted to sound out all but two of them ('skag' read as 'stick' and 'nos' read as nonsense). In addition, his phonic attempts were usually close to the targets, i.e. 'pad' read as 'ped'; 'lep' read as 'leg'; 'prit' read as 'pit'. He could not read any of the more difficult nonwords. His nonword reading confirmed that Harry was beginning to learn to apply letter–sound correspondences but needed instruction in blending. In addition his appreciation of letter–sound correspondences was limited to some single consonants (twenty-one in twenty-six correct). He knew only a few letter names (eleven in twenty-six correct). He was not yet familiar with consonant digraphs such as 'ch', 'th', consonant blends such as 'pl', 'bl', 'sw' and knew the sounds of only a few short vowels and vowel digraphs. Attempts to sound out words were therefore almost invariably doomed to failure. He not only had a weak grasp of sound–letter rules but in addition was completely unable to blend speech sounds correctly. In conclusion, he needed explicit instruction on grapheme–phoneme correspondences, blending and identifying words which corresponded to the results of the sounds he had blended.

Harry could not read any of the words on the regularity test included in this chapter but he was able to read seven regular and two irregular items on a much easier regularity test. There was therefore some evidence of emerging sensitivity to letter–sound mappings. Considering that his word recognition was also extremely poor, Harry needed to learn as much as possible about letter–sound relationships so that phonic information could be used to support word recognition.[19]

## Assessing phonological skills

Many tests have been devised to assess phonological skills, the ability to identify and manipulate speech sounds or phonemes. However, only a few of these are sensitive measures over a number of years.[20] The most useful appear to be rhyme production, sound categorization and word repetition.

## Rhyme production

Rhyme production, in which a child is asked to generate rhyming words or nonwords within a given span of time (generally 30 s), has proved to be a more sensitive instrument than rhyme recognition tests. The child is instructed to think of as many words or nonsense words as possible which rhyme with the target word. See table 4.3 for a version of a rhyme production test.[21] The percentage of correct responses is calculated. A child who makes a high proportion of errors, wandering extensively from the rime (the rhyming portion of the word), or who is unable to produce rhymes after the age of 7 is likely to have phonological processing difficulties.

Harry, for example, had substantial difficulty with this task even though he made only one error on a rhyme recognition test and performed perfectly on the Bradley Test of Auditory Organization.[22] He could usually think of one correct rhyme when he commenced the task, but he soon began to stray from the target word even though he was reminded of it after each incorrect response. For example, for the target 'jam' he responded with 'ham, man, can, flan, hand, man'. When comparing his performance with that of reading age matched controls, it was evident that Harry had severe phonological difficulties and that he needed explicit instruction in phonology and in relating the sounds in words to the letters used in written language.[23]

*Table 4.3*  Rhyme production

Instructions: I will give you a word and then I would like you to tell me as many words as you can which rhyme with it. Try and think of as many words or silly make-believe words as you can until I tell you to stop.

Trial 1: dog
Trial 2: cat

  1  bee
  2  play
  3  glue
  4  cook
  5  pie
  6  ball
  7  friend
  8  clown
  9  star
10  jam
11  snow
12  pig
13  dot
14  mice
15  bump
16  bunny
17  mitten
18  hopping
19  leather
20  cartoon

## Auditory organization

Lynette Bradley's Test of Auditory Organization[22] is a popular test of sound categorization which has been widely used in the past decade as a measure of phonological awareness. The child is asked to listen to a series of four words and to identify the 'odd one out', the word which differs from the other three, i.e. 'sun', 'gun', 'rub', 'fun'. Five-year-old children find 'odd one out items' which differ from the others in their initial consonants easier to detect than when the difference is in the final consonant.[24] Younger children who are having difficulties learning to read find this task difficult[25] but older children with reading difficulties are often able to perform it competently.[20] However, if the same task is presented but the items are altered so that the words are phonetically similar, differing only by one or two phonetic features such as voicing (/p/ and /b/; /t/ and /d/), i.e. 'pad, cab, dab, stab' or 'dot, hot, cot, pod', and/or place of articulation (/p/ and /t/; /t/ and /k/; /d/ and /b/), i.e. 'heat, wheat, leap, treat' or 'date, cake, state, wait', many children with reading problems have substantially more difficulty identifying the 'odd man out' than younger children with the same reading age.[26]

## Word and nonword repetition

Children who have problems identifying the component sound segments in words often have difficulties repeating polysyllabic words, particularly words they have never heard before.[27] This is because many of the same phonological processes are involved when one attempts to repeat an unfamiliar word as when one is undertaking other phonological tasks. One way of detecting such a difficulty is to ask individuals to repeat complex words and nonwords. One such list, developed by Snowling et al.,[4] is given in table 4.4. Most children aged 7 or above are able to repeat almost all the items correctly.

Harry, however, only repeated eight in twelve words and seven in twelve nonwords correctly. This performance was significantly below the norms for children with a reading age of 7. For example, he repeated 'hazardous' as 'hadzazas', 'spaghetti' as 'sagetti' and on a second attempt as 'pasgetti', and 'adebole' as 'adevolee'. The knock-on effect of difficulties with repetition needs to be stressed. Children who have difficulties repeating unfamiliar words will take longer to learn the correct pronunciations of new words and after a number of years are likely to have a poorer spoken vocabulary than children who repeat words accurately. Consequently, phonological difficulties may in the long run affect a child's performance not only on literacy tasks but on a number of spoken language tasks as well.

*Table 4.4*   Word and nonword repetition

The following words and nonwords can be presented for verbal repetition in random order. The nonwords should be pronounced by analogy to the real words from which they were derived, retaining stress as far as possible. Responses should be recorded as precisely as possible.

| *Words* | *Nonwords* |
|---|---|
| enemy | ineby |
| eskimo | istibo |
| melanie | beladie |
| anemone | adebole |
| buttercup | muddercup |
| slippery | swibbery |
| hazardous | bassarpus |
| spaghetti | skappedi |
| ambulance | andurant |
| christopher | gristother |
| statistics | spapistics |
| instructed | inspructid |

**Control data**
Number of correct responses (maximum, 12)

| *Reading age* | *Words* | *Nonwords* |
|---|---|---|
| 7 years | | |
| Mean | 11.25 | 10.83 |
| SD | 1.1 | 1.5 |
| Range | 9–12 | 7–12 |
| 10 years | | |
| Mean | 11.75 | 11.75 |
| SD | 0.6 | 0.5 |
| Range | 10–12 | 11–12 |

*Source*: Snowling, M.J., Stackhouse, J. and Rack, J.P. (1986) 'Phonological dyslexia and dysgraphia: a developmental analysis', *Cognitive Neuropsychology*, 3, 309–39

# Reading in Context

## Comprehension

The ability to understand or comprehend a text is undoubtedly the most critical component of reading. A child who can identify all the words in a story but cannot understand what he reads cannot be deemed to be reading. Such severe comprehension difficulties lie primarily in the domain of language and the teacher will wish to determine whether the child is able to understand the same material when it is read to the child. If listening comprehension is also poor,[28] the child should be referred to a speech and language therapist for an in-depth assessment of language skills (see chapter 6 for further discussion). Frequently, however, teachers find that listening comprehension skills are adequate or, on occasion, surprisingly good, and that the child's comprehension difficulties occur only when the text is too difficult and attention has to be shared between deciphering and understanding.

We have used the Neale Analysis of Reading Ability[29] for assessing reading comprehension. In this assessment children are requested to read a prose passage aloud and are told that they will be asked questions about the passage when they have read it. Three reading ages can be calculated at the end of the test. A reading accuracy age, a reading comprehension age and a reading rate age. When administering this test the examiner is required to supply a word if the reader is unable to read it and to correct any errors whilst the individual is reading. Comprehension and reading accuracy are, of course, not always in step. Some readers attain low reading accuracy scores and substantially higher comprehension scores because word recognition errors are constantly corrected. Other children recognize individual words competently and achieve a good score on reading accuracy but nevertheless have severe difficulties in understanding what they have read.

Simon was almost 10 years old when he was referred because of severe spoken and written language comprehension difficulties despite a normal verbal IQ and a superior performance IQ as measured on the WISC-R. Although chatty and communicative, he found a change of subject disconcerting and was slow to tune in to the new topic. Reading accuracy score on the Neale Analysis of Reading Ability was 11 years 1 month and spelling ability was also excellent. He spelled twenty three- and four-syllable words making few, minor spelling errors.

His receptive vocabulary assessed on the British Picture Vocabulary Scale was also within the normal range. In contrast to his good comprehension for single words he had extreme difficulties defining words – even such common words as 'sport', 'army', 'beard' and 'invite'. More striking was the manner in which he struggled to express his ideas. When asked to recall a story he managed to relate the beginning but needed prompting to remember what happened subsequently and completely omitted the conclusion. Likewise when asked to sequence six pictures so that they told a story and then to explain the story, his spoken version was simplistic and was characterized by immature use of grammar.

He attained a reading comprehension age on the Neale Analysis of 8 years 10 months, clearly well below that expected from his word reading accuracy scores and below the norm for his chronological age. Understanding even the easy passages posed problems despite the fact that he read them virtually without errors. As the passages became more difficult his errors became increasingly inappropriate due to his inability to make semantically suitable substitutions. For example, he read the phrase 'recent mishap' as 'recent mishape' and 'in peril' as 'in pearl'. His infrequent reading errors were clearly associated with severe comprehension problems. He could answer fewer than 50 per cent of the comprehension questions correctly.

Simon needs more explicit instruction in comprehension, with attention paid to both oral and written language. An attempt to expand vocabulary skills and to help Simon consider the characteristic defining features of words would also be beneficial. Cloze procedure (passages in which words are omitted at recurrent intervals) would be an invaluable way of showing Simon that it is possible to predict missing words from the information already supplied in the text. Exercises in which alternative adjectives, verbs or adverbs completely alter the meaning of the test can also be an amusing way to encourage vocabulary development. (For further discussion of the remediation of comprehension difficulties see chapter 6.)

## Using context to help word recognition

It is also necessary to consider children whose comprehension skills are within the normal range but who have not as yet realized that reading for meaning can be an extremely useful adjunct when they are having difficulty identifying a word or making sense of text. Readers whose word recognition skills and/or recoding skills are as yet poorly developed should be encouraged to use contextual information whenever possible. Although it is essential to teach poor recoders the fundamental alphabetic principles which underlie the English spelling system, many children with poor phonological skills will never become proficient recoders. (See for example the case of J.M.[16]) Encouraging 'reading for meaning', whilst concurrently paying attention to graphemic cues, will in most cases greatly improve reading attainment.

Harry (who you may recall was 8 years 6 months old at this time) was an example of a child who was not yet taking advantage of his good comprehension skills. He obtained a reading accuracy score of 6 years 10 months and a comprehension score of 6 years 9 months on the Neale Analysis of Reading Ability (1958) Form A. He made many visually based errors even on the easiest passage. He misread 'came' as 'called', 'went' as 'wailed', 'her' as 'the', 'now' as 'not'. Although his comprehension score was in line with his accuracy score, it was evident that he rarely used context to help him identify words. On the second passage Harry was able to answer seven out of eight comprehension questions despite the fact that he made over seventeen accuracy errors. The passage with Harry's errors printed in italics is reproduced below (the abbreviation [Ref] stands for refusal):

| | *sat* | *the* | [Ref] | | *he* | | | *stopped* | *has* |
|---|---|---|---|---|---|---|---|---|---|
| | Tom | stopped | on his way to school. The milkman's | | | horse | | had |

| *walked* | *up* | *field.* | | *house* | | *went* |
|---|---|---|---|---|---|---|
| wandered | in the | fog. | The | horse | and cart | blocked the |

| */k/* | | *can* | *want* | | *this* | *were* | *traffic* |
|---|---|---|---|---|---|---|---|
| centre | of the road. | Traffic | was | coming. | There | was no | time |

| | *come* | | *quick* | | *had left* | | [Ref] |
|---|---|---|---|---|---|---|---|
| to | call | the milkman. | Quickly | Tom led | | the horse to | safety |

| [Ref] | [Ref] | | [Ref] |
|---|---|---|---|
| just as the frightened | | milkman | returned. |

Perhaps the most obvious conclusion is that Harry is unable to read this passage. If he had not been receiving constant feedback about his errors he would probably not have answered any of the comprehension questions correctly. The majority of his word recognition errors used first letter cues only, i.e. 'stopped' read as 'sat', 'fog' read as 'field', 'was' read as 'were', 'was' read as 'want', 'time' read as 'traffic', 'call' read as 'come'. A few errors incorporated more extensive letter information, i.e. 'wandered' read as 'walked', 'horse' read as 'house'. Some errors did not even take account of initial letters, i.e. 'his' read as 'the', 'he' read as 'the', 'in' read as 'up', 'blocked' read as 'went', 'traffic' read as 'can'. (Note that once again Harry guesses a word which begins with the final letter of the written word.) In addition, few errors were semantically correct although the picture of the milkman and his horse which accompanied the passage had provided essential information. It is clear that Harry has not yet understood about reading for meaning but that considering his overall good comprehension of the passage he should be able to adopt such a strategy with success if given appropriate instruction. Although his recoding ability is still limited, he should also be encouraged to use initial sound cues to constrain his guesses.


## Spelling

Although this chapter focuses on the assessment of reading, clinical experience has convinced us that it is imperative to investigate spelling for an accurate appraisal of the cognitive skills required for reading. Spelling is initially more dependent on phonological skills than reading. In the early stages of spelling, children rely primarily on their pronunciation of words when trying to work out how words should be spelled[30] – hence the close relationship between spelling and phonological skills.[31] Second, English is an alphabetic language. In order to arrive at some understanding of the underlying logic of English spelling the child has to come to the realization that letters represent speech sounds or phonemes. Once beginners have managed to understand this vital link between spoken and written language, they can begin to invent intelligible spellings. A few beginners produce unintelligible spellings which do not sound in any way like the words they are attempting to write. Sometimes this occurs simply because a child's grasp of letter names or sounds is poor. However, unintelligible spelling is most frequently the consequence of underlying phonological deficits. Children who have difficulties identifying and distinguishing between speech sounds or phonemes are less likely to recognize that certain letters map onto a particular speech sound. Consequently, these children are unable to learn letter–sound rules even when they are taught to the whole class.

In general little attention is paid to children whose reading skills appear to be within the normal range but who spell poorly. This is unfortunate because poor spelling reflects more serious processing difficulties and should be given adequate consideration. A child who is able to rely on context and sight words may appear to be developing normally in the early years despite the fact that phonological skills may be seriously impaired. Moreover, these children often display reading difficulties at a later stage when they encounter new words which cannot be identified through context and phonic recoding becomes the only strategy which makes word identification possible.

Two simple tests can be used to assess spelling: a standardized spelling test with subsequent error analysis and a free-writing exercise. The simplest and often the most informative of these is free-writing. A piece of writing lasting approximately ten minutes should suffice for an initial assessment.

## Free writing

Initially the writing should be examined for the following points.

1  Intelligibility: is it possible to understand the content without asking the child to provide additional information? Is the child able to read back what has been written? Often poor spellers have only vague impressions of what they intended to write and are unable to reread their own writing.
2  Taking into account the standard of the rest of the class is this piece of writing above average, average or substantially below average?
3  If spelling is well below average it is essential to perform a

detailed error analysis in order to identify weaknesses and to investigate which strategies the child is using. A simple way of analysing spelling errors is to classify them as phonetic, partially phonetic, non-phonetic. Phonetic spellings sound like the word the speller is trying to spell, for example 'pupy', 'parst', 'bort', 'sed', 'shuvel'. A partially phonetic spelling contains the correct consonants but the vowels are omitted or are incorrect, i.e. 'ran' for 'run'; 'hay' for 'high'; 'lcke' for 'like'. A non-phonetic spelling error does not sound like the word it was intended to be and cannot be identified by a reader without contextual information, for example 'pleol' for 'people', 'ayesy' for 'ask'; 'hmumot' for 'house'; 'pletne' for 'people'; 'flaum' for 'family'.

In general, beginners' errors are initially non-phonetic, gradually becoming increasingly phonetic. Learners also begin to incorporate an increasing amount of word-specific knowledge in their spellings. It is possible to classify poor spellers into two groups. The first group have severe phonological difficulties and tend to use a large number of non-phonetic errors when their peers are producing phonetic spellings which sound much more like the target. (See for example the spellings of J.M.[16]) The second group of poor spellers are able to use phonetic spelling but have excessive difficulty remembering the correct spellings of words. They tend to spell mainly by sound, having particular difficulties spelling irregular words or words which require exact spelling information such as the presence of a double consonant or the spelling of homophones (e.g. steak and stake) (see for example the spellings of J.A.S.[5]).

Harry was given a simple cartoon about a bird that falls out of its nest and is found by a dog and was asked to write the story. He was told that he had to finish in ten minutes but should try to spend all that time on the task. He wrote:

A NES IN A TEER AND A BRAD FOT AND A BOG CUD TO HIS MUS THE DOR SLIT THE TRE A POT THE BAT BAC.

He read it back as 'A nest in a tree and a bird fell out and a dog called to his master. The boy climbed the tree and put the bird back.'

It is evident from this piece that although he has learned to spell a few simple words ('a', 'in', 'and', 'to', 'his') he has little understanding of how to 'invent' spellings and relies instead on visual memory ('teer' and 'tre' for 'tree') and on first letter cues.

## Standardized spelling test

A standardized spelling test is valuable because it not only provides an objective measure of how the child performs in comparison to other children of the same age, but in addition lends itself to error analysis so that inferences can be made about the child's spelling strategies.

Harry's spelling age on the Vernon Graded Word Spelling Test[32] was 6 years 2 months. Apart from the words he spelled correctly (is, see, up, red, gun and sick) most of Harry's spellings were non-phonetic: 'am' was spelled 'amn'; 'do' was spelled 'drow'; 'down' was spelled 'dunb'. These errors demonstrate a very basic difficulty with phonetic analysis and sound-to-letter transcription. Although Harry has begun to acquire alphabetic skills these errors reveal that they are still far from proficient and it will be necessary for him to be given explicit instruction to encourage the transfer of encoding skills to reading.

In contrast, Dan produced the following errors: 'littal'; 'hork'; 'pepel'; 'bom'; 'tuch'; 'air' (heir); 'rime'; 'sine'; 'butte'. The preponderance of phonetically plausible misspellings reveals that he has mastered encoding but that he has severe difficulties with lexical information. Unlike Harry, Dan needs to concentrate on learning word families which contain specific letter patterns as for example 'aw' ('saw', 'raw', 'jaw', 'lawn', 'hawk'), 'oy' ('boy', 'joy'), 'ew' (new, threw). He particularly needs to be taught the irregular words he uses frequently, i.e. 'beauty', 'sign', 'people', and should be helped to find which method he finds most effective for learning them (see Goulandris[33] for alternative ways of learning irregular words).

## Case Study

Peter was 7 years 10 months when he was first seen. He had had delayed speech development and was initially intelligible only to his mother. There was also a strong family history of reading difficulties and language delay.

On the Neale Analysis of Reading Ability (1966) Peter scored an accuracy reading age approximately 2 years below his current age. He recognized only a few of the words in the passages and made many visually based errors, confusing words which were only somewhat visually similar. For example, he read 'can' as 'cow', 'car' as 'cat' and 'if' as 'let' (based on the similar shape of the uppercase 'I' and the lowercase 'l'). Peter made almost no use of context to help him identify words or to enable him to monitor the plausibility of his reading. He read 'I am in a car' as 'I aim in a cat' without any indication that he felt uncomfortable with his rendition. Clearly, in his mind reading did not need to make much sense!

Peter's single word reading was at a very elementary level. He recognized only two of the words on the BAS Test of Word Reading. He was unable to read any of the regular and irregular words listed above. Phonic ability was also rudimentary. He was only able to read three in ten one-syllable nonwords. His knowledge of letter–sound rules was poor and he was unable to blend speech sounds in order to form a word. Phonic skills were therefore virtually non-existent for reading. Letter knowledge was also poor. He could only name eleven letters correctly and knew few letter–sound correspondences.

Articulation was still immature. He mispronounced the speech sounds /w/ and /r/ and the more commonly confused pair /f/ and /th/. He had no difficulty with rhyme decision tasks and was moderately proficient at producing rhymes when given an exemplar. Occasionally he switched from producing rhyming responses to completely incorrect responses, i.e. for the target 'can' he produced the responses 'jam', 'fam', 'joke', 'jack', 'jam' and for the target 'dot' after producing a number of correct rhymes he volunteered 'lock', 'gob' and 'slob', showing some fundamental phoneme confusions even though the target word was repeated to him after each incorrect response.

Peter's free-writing showed that he had severe problems with writing and generally could not use phonological information to guide his spelling attempts. When asked to write a story depicted in the cartoon showing a baby bird which falls out of his nest and the dog who takes the bird to its owner, Peter produced the following:

TOU LIC FEL ART OV TOU TOU IXEX TOXU DOG SNIKI IR PII.

When he 'read back' what he thought he'd written the discrepancy between his competent oral version and unintelligible written version was striking. It was therefore not surprising that he was completely unable to spell any of the words on the Vernon Spelling Test correctly.

When seen two years later at 9 years 10 months Peter's reading age was still 2 years below his chronological age but he had made the normal rate of progress, i.e. two years' progress in two years. On the BAS Test of Reading he attained a reading age of 7 years 3 months. The important question was whether Peter was making better use of the three types of reading strategies.

Single word reading had improved although he was still relying heavily on approximate visual recognition, i.e. 'ceiling' read as 'cooling', 'writing' as 'wedding'. However, his visual errors now incorporated more graphemic information than previously, i.e. 'light' read as 'lit' and 'lift'; 'coat' read as 'cat'; 'carpet' read as 'carping' and 'switch' read as 'witch' – an important step forward. Unsuccessful phonic attempts had also substantially increased on a variety of single word reading tests, indicating greater awareness of the possibility of sublexical processing when contextual cues were unavailable, i.e. 'invite' was read as 'inverterer'; 'enemy' as 'any my'; 'favour' as 'farven'; 'drab' as 'draben'. There was also evidence of regularizations, i.e. 'ache' read as 'atch', 'prove' as 'proav', 'shoe' as 'show'. Thus single word reading was now taking account of both letter and letter–sound information and although both lexical and sublexical processing were still immature they had begun to develop. He was also able to read seventeen regular and nine irregular words performing completely in line with normally developing controls with a reading age of 7.

On the Neale Analysis of Reading Ability (1958) Form B[34] it was evident that Peter was often able to use meaning to restrict his selection of words which were visually similar to the target word. In the first passage which reads

Then out jumped a white rabbit

he read

*Then one jumped a weird rabbit.*

The beginning of passage 2 reads

John and Ann were fishing. Suddenly they heard a splash. A woods-man had fallen into the lake. He could not swim for he was hurt. The children tried to pull him ashore. Then John held the man's head above water and Ann ran for help.

Peter read this portion as

*John and Ann were fishing. Suddenly they <u>had</u> a splash. A woodsman had fallen into the <u>water</u>. He <u>called</u> not swim for he was hurt. The children tried to pull him <u>out</u>. He was too . . .*

The last sentence was too difficult for Peter and he was totally unable to grasp the correct meaning, reading the sentence as '*Then John <u>had</u> the man's <u>hard</u> <u>ad</u> water*'. Several of these errors were clearly influenced by context. For example, his version 'A woods-man had fallen into the water' was a totally appropriate semantic substitution for the correct phrase 'the lake'. His next error, 'He called', also makes sense. If you fall in the water, you are likely to call for help. It also takes into account a number of the letter cues present in the target word 'could'. The next error is once again an example of an acceptable substitution. Instead of the correct 'The children tried to pull him ashore', Peter substituted the word 'ashore' with the word 'out'. So Peter's responses are now to a great extent constrained by his interpretation of the passage.

Despite a relatively mediocre reading accuracy performance, he made no errors on the comprehension questions on this passage.

However, as the passages became more difficult he was increasingly reluctant to attempt unfamiliar words. His errors shifted from semantically correct and context based to unrelated visual errors. He read 'arranging' as 'around', 'new' as 'now', 'appear' as 'apart', 'choice' as 'chick'. None of these misreadings made sense within the context of the passage in which they occurred. For the three passages read, totalling 147 words, there was only one attempt to sound out a word he did not recognize immediately. He scored an overall Reading Age Accuracy score of 7 years 8 months and a Reading Comprehension Age of 8 years 5 months, demonstrating better comprehension than word identification ability.

Nonword reading remained weak but was no longer outside the normal range. He was now able to read six in ten simple nonwords and ten in twenty-two more difficult ones.

Thus Peter's strategies had shifted over the two-year period. Use of contextual cues had improved substantially but still needed refinement. There were also improvements in phonic strategies as seen in his improved nonword reading. However, as he never used phonics spontaneously when reading text, he had not been able to incorporate phonics into his reading. This second assessment gives clear indication that Peter is gradually developing more balanced reading strategies. His teachers now need to help him integrate them so that they can be used spontaneously whilst reading text.

Finally spelling skills had also improved substantially and he was producing more correct spelling and more phonologically plausible errors than on the previous occasion (figure 4.1).

In conclusion, we have found that assessing reading development in terms of three basic reading components, word recognition, phonic recoding and comprehension, can be invaluable. Producing a reading profile for each child with reading difficulties enables teachers to identify untapped underlying strengths and can often result in dramatic improvements in reading skills. A clear understanding of a child's weaknesses is also essential. Although many more longitudinal studies need to be carried out before firm conclusions can be drawn about the prognosis of children with reading difficulties and the choice of the most effective teaching approach, it is likely that the most progress will occur when an individualized teaching programme is devised which gives

at home We have lots of animels. we have for dog
and thay names are Hune Cloe Leo and Samsoon
and a bue cold Snoe and for gots to ofthem
are cold pope and

*Figure 4.1*    Peter's free writing

priority to developing proficient cognitive abilities while still attempting to remedy deficits.

NOTES

1   Adams, M.J. 1990: *Beginning to Read*, Cambridge, MA: MIT Press.
2   Snowling, M.J. 1987: *Dyslexia. A Cognitive Developmental Perspective*, Oxford:
    Basil Blackwell.
3   Frith, U. and Snowling, M. 1983: 'The role of sound, shape and ortho-
    graphic cues in early reading', *British Journal of Psychology*, 72, 83–7.
4   Snowling, M.J., Stackhouse, J. and Rack, J.P. 1986: 'Phonological dyslexia
    and dysgraphia: a developmental analysis', *Cognitive Neuropsychology*, 3, 309–
    39.
5   Goulandris, N. K. and Snowling, M. 1991: 'Visual memory deficits: a plaus-
    ible cause of developmental dyslexia? Evidence from a single case study',
    *Cognitive Neuropsychology*, 8, 127–54.
6   Stroop, J.R. 1935: 'Studies of interference in serial verbal reactions', *Journal
    of Experimental Psychology*, 18, 643–62.
7   Goodman, K.S. 1967: 'Reading: a psycholinguistic guessing game', *Journal
    of the Reading Specialist*, May, 126–35.
8   Smith, F. 1971: *Understanding Reading: A Psycholinguistic Analysis of Reading
    and Learning to Read*, New York: Holt, Rinehart and Winston.
9   Stanovich, K.E. 1980: 'Toward an interactive-compensatory model of indi-
    vidual differences in the development of reading fluency', *Reading Research
    Quarterly*, 16, 32–71.
10  Macmillan Test Unit 1985: *Macmillan Graded Word Reading Test*, Basingstoke:
    Macmillan Educational.
11  Schonell, F.J. 1971: *Graded Word Reading Test*, Edinburgh: Oliver and Boyd.
12  Frith, U. 1985: 'Beneath the surface of developmental dyslexia', in K.E.
    Patterson, M. Coltheart and J.C. Marshall (eds), *Surface Dyslexia: Neuro-
    psychological and Cognitive Studies of Phonological Reading*, London: Lawrence
    Erlbaum Associates.
13  Elliott, C.D., Murray, D.J. and Pearson, L.S. 1983: *British Ability Scales*,
    Windsor: NFER-Nelson.

14   Stuart, M. and Coltheart, M. 1988: 'Does reading develop in a sequence of stages?', *Cognition*, 30, 139–81.

15   Bradley, L. and Bryant, P. 1983: 'Categorising sounds and learning to read: a causal connection', *Nature*, 301, 419.

16   Snowling, M.J. and Hulme, C. 1989: 'A longitudinal case study of developmental phonological dyslexia', *Cognitive Neuropsychology*, 6, 379–401.

17   Rack, J.P., Snowling, M.J. and Olson, R.K. 1992: ' The nonword reading deficit in developmental dyslexia: a review', *Reading Research Quarterly*, 27, 28–53.

18   Goswami, U. 1988: 'Orthographic analogies and reading development', *Quarterly Journal of Experimental Psychology*, 40A, 239–68.

19   Ehri, L. 1985: 'Sources of difficulty in learning to spell and read', in M.L. Wolraich and D. Routh (eds), *Advances in Developmental and Behavioural Paediatrics*, vol. 7, Greenwich, CT: JAI Press, 121–95.

20   Snowling, Goulandris and Defty, submitted.

21   Goulandris, A. (1989) Emergent spelling: The development of spelling strategies in young children. Unpublished thesis. University College London, University of London.

22   Bradley, L. 1980: *Assessing Reading Difficulties*, London: Macmillan Educational.

23   Hatcher, P., Hulme, C. and Ellis, A.W. 1994: 'Ameliorating early reading failure by integrating the teaching of reading and phonological skills: the phonological linkage hypothesis', *Child Development*, 65, 41–57.

24   Kirtley, C., Bryant, P., Maclean, M. and Bradley, L. 1989: 'Rhyme, rime, and the onset of reading', *Journal of Experimental Child Psychology*, 48, 224–45.

25   Bradley, L. and Bryant, P. 1978: 'Difficulties in auditory organization as a possible cause of reading backwardness', *Nature*, 271, 746–7.

26   Snowling, M.J., Hulme, C., Smith, A., Thomas, J., 1994: 'The effects of phonetic similarity and list length on children's sound categorization performance', *Journal of Experimental Child Psychology*, 58, 160–80.

27   Snowling, M.J., Goulandris, N., Bowlby, M. and Howell, P. 1986: 'Segmentation and speech perception in relation to reading skill: a developmental analysis', *Journal of Experimental Child Psychology*, 41, 489–507.

28   Stanovich, K.E. 1991: 'The theoretical and practical consequences of discrepancy definitions of dyslexia', in M. Snowling and M. Thomson (eds), *Dyslexia. Integrating Theory and Practice*, London: Whurr.

29   Neale, Marie 1966: *Neale Analysis of Reading Ability*, 2nd edn, London: Macmillan Educational.

30   Read, C. 1986: *Children's Creative Spelling*, London: Routledge and Kegan Paul.

31   Perin, D. 1983: 'Phonemic segmentation and spelling', *British Journal of Psychology*, 74, 129–44.

32   Vernon, P.E. 1977: *Graded Word Spelling Test*, London: Hodder and Stoughton.

33   Goulandris, N. 1990: 'Children with spelling problems', in P. Pinsent (ed.), *Children with Literacy Difficulties*, London: David Fulton.

34   See note 29.

# 5

# *Helping to Overcome Early Reading Failure by Combining the Teaching of Reading and Phonological Skills*

Peter J. Hatcher, Charles Hulme and Andrew W. Ellis

*As Roger Beard points out in chapter 1, theories of teaching reading and the practice of teaching reading in the classroom often differ. Experienced teachers have tried-and-tested methods of teaching reading and of remedial teaching that they know achieve success. They do not need an educationalist or experimental psychologist to tell them so.*

*Nevertheless, it is difficult to know for certain what it is about the method a particular teacher practises that leads to its success. A variety of approaches may be used, some of which may be more helpful than others; the way in which a method is used may be more important than the method itself; some teachers may simply be more encouraging than others and the methods used may be unimportant. It is here that the approach of the experimental psychologist can be helpful. By investigating different approaches to the teaching of reading in a systematic manner, carefully controlling other factors which might be important but are not to do with the method itself, it should be possible to assess the effects of particular approaches, pinpointing the aspects which are beneficial so that an objective measure of the usefulness of a particular method can be obtained.*

In the study reported in this chapter, Peter Hatcher, Charles Hulme and Andrew Ellis assess an integrated training programme to improve the reading of a group of 7-year-old children who were failing to learn to read at the normal rate. The programme involved over twenty teachers working in seventeen different schools. It involved training in visual reading strategies and phonology, and the authors were particularly interested to know which aspect of the programme contributed most to learning: visual reading, phonology or the combination of both.

They found that children who fail to read are more likely to benefit from an integrated programme than from isolated training in either visual reading strategies or in phonological awareness. This is an important finding and may apply to the great majority of children with reading difficulties. The study shows that if we are to understand what children need to know in order to learn to read, and how best to teach this knowledge, then we need to carry out careful experiments in which the different aspects of a method are systematically controlled. These experiments do not need to be conducted in artificial circumstances but can be conducted in schools, without interfering with the normal course of a child's learning experience.

## Introduction

Over the past three decades, psychologists studying early reading development have devoted much of their energies to studying the relationship between progress in reading and the possession of what are known as 'phonological skills' (or 'phonological awareness'). These two terms, which tend to be used interchangeably, refer to a child's ability to identify, reflect upon and manipulate the sounds of spoken language. A variety of tasks have been used to assess phonological skill. Children may, for example, be asked to split words up into their component syllables or individual speech sounds (referred to as 'phonemes'), dividing 'window' into 'win' and 'dow' or 'dog' into 'd', 'o' and 'g' (so-called 'phoneme segmentation'). They may be asked to count the numbers of syllables or phonemes in a word, or to delete syllables or phonemes from words and say what remains after the deletion (e.g. removing the 's' from 'spin' to make 'pin'). They may be asked to blend syllables or phonemes together to form words, or to say whether two words rhyme. Another frequently used task requires children to identify the 'odd word out' in sets of words, all but one of which share a common sound. For example, in the set of words 'pin, sit, win, fin', three words share the rhyme 'in', so 'sit' is the odd word out. This task is one of three that Lynette Bradley and Peter Bryant[1] in Oxford refer to collectively as 'sound categorization'. The other two sound categorization tasks involve identifying words with a different medial sound (e.g. 'hat' in 'lot, cot, pot, hat') and identifying words with a different initial sound (e.g. 'rug' in 'bun, bud, rug, bus').

The relationship between phonological skill and reading ability may be assessed by testing children's phonological ability at the same time as their reading skills, or by assessing phonological ability and then seeing how children with different levels of phonological skill subsequently progress in their reading. Such research has produced a mass of evidence linking the development of children's reading skills to their underlying phonological skills. Even when possible differences in intelligence between children with good or poor phonological ability have been taken into account, performance on phonological awareness tasks is among the best predictors of success in learning to read.

An implication of this finding is that it might be possible to enhance reading progress, or in some instances to prevent reading delay, by improving young children's phonological awareness. It is not quite as simple as that, however. The fact that phonological skill predicts progress in literacy does not prove conclusively that phonological skill contributes to success in learning to read, and demonstrating that improving phonological skill improves reading does not prove conclusively that one causes the other. The relationship between the two sets of skills may be due to the influence of some third factor. For example, the child who is taken aside for individual training in phonological skill may develop a more positive attitude towards classroom work in general, and this may be why his or her reading improves. This is an important consideration since, if the relationship between phonological skill and reading development is not a direct one, there might be little point in putting time and effort into teaching phonological skills to young children.

If one could establish beyond reasonable doubt that training in phonological skills helps children learn to read, it then becomes important to know whether this happens when the phonological training is done using speech alone or whether it is necessary for children to be explicitly taught how to apply their phonological skills in reading. For example, if children are taught to segment words, delete phonemes and spot rhymes using pictures and spoken words as materials, will this alone help them to learn to read, or do they have to be shown how the phonemes and syllables of spoken words are represented by letters and letter groups in written words before they can bring their phonological skills to bear on the business of reading?

As we shall see, there is in fact little evidence that phonological training which does not relate the structure of speech to the structure of writing has much effect on learning to read. There is, in contrast, growing evidence that phonological skills training affects progress in literacy when it is integrated with the teaching of reading. One of the purposes of this chapter is to describe a study[2] we have carried out to look at the relationship between phonological training and the teaching of reading. In the study, three groups of children were given three different types of training. One group received phonological skills training alone. These children were taught to segment, delete, blend and so on, but the teaching involved only spoken words: children in this group were not explicitly shown how the sounds of spoken English relate to the letters of written English. A second group received training in reading skills, but their training was stripped of all reference to what would traditionally be called 'phonics'. The third group received some pure phonological training and some pure reading training, but were also taught how to relate these two together. The results provide strong support for the effectiveness of combining phonological skills training with early literacy teaching and have important implications for the way that we teach reading. In view of the positive nature of the results we obtained, another purpose of the chapter is to provide details about the training procedures used in our study. We hope they will be of help to teachers and others concerned with the development of early literacy in children.

## The Phonological Linkage Hypothesis

Before describing our study in detail, we will briefly review some of the previous work in this area, work that led us to formulate the hypothesis about the relationship between phonological skill and reading that underpinned our work – what we call the 'phonological linkage hypothesis'. One of the most influential studies of the relationship between learning to read and phonological awareness is that carried out by Lynette Bradley and Peter Bryant.[1] They selected sixty-five 5- to 6-year-old children, who had been poor at sound categorization as 4- to 5-year-old pre-readers, and split them into four groups. Two groups (groups 1 and 2) were trained in sound categorization using pictures (e.g. bag, bed, boat and bus). Group 1 was the group that Bradley and Bryant were particularly interested in. Group 2 (the first taught control group) was also taught to appreciate that, where a group of words shared common sounds, the sounds were represented by specific letters. Plastic letters were used to get this idea across to the members of group 2. Group 3, the second taught control group, was taught to categorize the pictures into conceptual groupings (e.g. things found in a house). If group 3 improved as much as groups 1 and 2, the improvements could be put down to general factors such as increased motivation rather than to specific effects of the sound categorization training. Group 4, an unseen control group, received no experimental training.

The training was spread over two years. By the end, group 1 was about four months ahead of group 3 in reading. However, the difference between the groups was not statistically significant. In contrast, group 2, which received both sound categorization and letter–sound correspondence training, was about eight to ten months ahead of group 3 in reading. This difference in progress is statistically significant. It is also an important finding in that it suggests that phonological training may be particularly effective in improving reading skills when it is combined with reading instruction. According to this view, training phonological skills in isolation from reading and spelling skills may be less effective than training that forms links between children's underlying phonological skills and their experiences in learning to read. We term this the 'phonological linkage hypothesis'.

There are three other important studies that are consistent with the phonological linkage hypothesis. One study was carried out in Umea, Sweden, by Ingvar Lundberg, Jorgen Frost and Ole-Peter Petersen.[3] Like Bradley and Bryant,[1] these researchers were interested in whether phonological training affects progress in learning to read. They gave a structured programme of general phonological activities to 235 Danish kindergarten children from the island of Bornholm. Children who were given this training before they started to learn to read turned out to be better at reading by the time they reached grade 2 than children who had not received such training. The effect of the training on reading skills was small, however, suggesting once again that phonological skills training which is divorced from the teaching of reading is not a powerful way of improving reading development.

Another study by Anne Cunningham[4] in Berkeley, California, gave two groups of kindergarten and first-grade children two forms of phonemic awareness training. Group 1 received training in phoneme segmentation and blending, while group 2 received training that, in addition, emphasized the link between phonemic awareness and reading. Cunningham found that, among the older children, those in group 2 made more progress in reading than those in group 1. This fits with the phonological linkage hypothesis. However, as with the Bradley and Bryant[1] study, it is possible that the greater progress of the group 2 children was due to the reading aspect of their training. It may not have been due to the integration of the phonological training and reading instruction.

The third training study is that carried out by Eileen Ball and Benita Blachman[5,6] in New York. Their study involved two groups of kindergarten children. Group 1 received training in sound categorization, phoneme segmentation, letter–name and letter–sound correspondence and a spell-by-sounds training package known as DISTAR. The second group received general language activity training in addition to letter–name and letter–sound training. The results, which are once again in line with the phonological linkage hypothesis, showed that the reading and spelling performance of group 1 improved more than that of group 2.

In addition to these training studies, there is evidence from a number of other studies that is consistent with the phonological linkage hypothesis. For example, William Tunmer, Michael Herriman and Andrew Nesdale[7] in Western Australia gave first-grade children a test of phoneme segmentation and a test which required them to read aloud invented 'nonwords' such as 'Mip' or 'Flug'. Because these strings of letters are new to all the children, this is a relatively pure measure of phonic reading skill. Tunmer and his colleagues found that all the children who performed well on the phonic reading task had good phonemic awareness skills. There were some children, however, who did well on the phoneme segmentation test but read nonwords poorly. Tunmer and his colleagues conclude that phonological awareness is necessary for the acquisition of phonic reading skill but is not sufficient: children must be taught how to apply their phonological awareness in reading if they are to gain the full benefit.

As discussed in chapter 2, a similar conclusion was drawn by Brian Byrne and Ruth Fielding-Barnsley[8] in New South Wales. They looked at the ability of young pre-literate children to understand the alphabetic principle; i.e. to demonstrate an understanding of the fact that particular phonemes in words are represented by particular letters. To examine this they first taught 3- to 5-year-old children to read the words 'mat' and 'sat'. The children were then asked to decide whether the printed word 'mow' should be pronounced as 'mow' or 'sow'. Byrne and Fielding-Barnsley found that this task was only reliably performed by children who understood (1) that 'm' is a separate component of 'mat', (2) that the 'm' sounds in 'mat' and 'mow' are the same, and (3) that the 'm' and 's' sounds are represented by particular letters. Byrne and Fielding-Barnsley concluded that 'neither phoneme awareness nor letter–sound knowledge was sufficient for acquisition of the alphabetic principle. They were needed in combination.' Reading and phonology must be linked.

## Research Design

The aim of our study was to test the phonological linkage hypothesis within a school setting and with children who were showing signs of difficulty in the early stages of learning to read. These are the children upon whom intervention might most profitably be targeted before their reading falls too far behind that of their class-mates. We wished to test whether an intervention that involved a combination of reading instruction and phonological training would be more effective in boosting children's reading skills than interventions that involved either reading instruction with pho-nology removed or phonological training alone. The study there-fore required the use of three experimental groups, one receiving each type of training. In addition, we needed an unseen control group against which the progress of the experimental groups could be contrasted.

The intervention took the form of two half-hour sessions of one-to-one training per week for twenty weeks. It is important to realize that we made no attempt to control the children's entire reading experience. All of the children received their normal teach-ing as part of their normal classroom work, but the children in the three experimental groups received two half-hours a week on top.

Our research design allowed us to assess whether training pho-nological skills alone is enough to improve the reading of poor readers. If this were the case, the reading of both groups given phonological training should improve. However, our phonologi-cal linkage hypothesis made the specific prediction that the chil-dren given an integrated combination of reading and phonological training would make more progress than any of the other groups. We did not have a group who spent two half-hours a week doing something irrelevant in order to show that gains in reading were not due to some general factor such as motivation. Instead, we assessed maths skill at the beginning and end of the intervention. Any non-specific improvement such as increased attention and effort in the classroom would show up in improved maths per-formance as much as in improved reading, whereas if we were training something specific to the reading process, maths should not be helped.

## Selecting the children

The starting point for the study was a county-wide survey of the reading of 6- to 7-year-olds in their third year of infant schooling in Cumbria Education Authority, United Kingdom. This screening used the Carver test,[9] a group administered single word reading test where children have to underline one of a group of words to match the word that has been spoken by the examiner. Following the survey, we identified 188 children as having reading quotients of less than 86 (where a quotient of 100 would be average). We screened them for severe general learning difficulties using the Raven's Coloured Progressive Matrices.[10] In this 'non-verbal' test children are presented with a design from which a part has been removed and have to choose a matching insert from one of six alternatives. We excluded twenty children whose performance on the Matrices test put them in the bottom 25 per cent of the population and whose Carver reading quotient was less than 71. Other children were excluded for a variety of reasons including failure to obtain parental consent to participate (six), change of school (nine) and being given legal entitlements to special educational provision (seven). From the remaining children, we selected 128 and divided them into four groups of thirty-two. These groups were matched on IQ, reading ability, age and sex (eighteen boys and fourteen girls in each group). For the purposes of matching groups, we used two verbal (similarities and vocabulary) and two performance (object assembly and block design) subtests of the Wechsler Intelligence Scale for Children – Revised[11] to estimate IQ. The British Ability Scales (BAS) Word Reading Test A[12] was used as the measure of reading ability. Subsequently, three children moved out of the area. This reduced the number of children in the study to 125 (see table 5.1). The remaining children showed a wide range of IQs (68–122) and can be considered representative of $7\frac{1}{2}$-year-old children experiencing reading problems. The children were spread across seventeen schools, each school having a balance of children in each group. We assigned poor readers from the same school to different groups so that group membership was not confounded with attendance at different schools (which could have different approaches to the teaching of reading).

After the matching and selection process, we assigned the four groups to one of three experimental conditions and a control condition. As already noted, these were reading with phonology (R+P), reading alone (R), phonology alone (P) and a control (C). By this time the children were all 7 years old. We chose to study

*Table 5.1* Means (average scores) for age, BAS word reading age and WISC-R Full-Scale IQ for the four groups (*N* = 124)

| Group | Age | Reading age | IQ |
|---|---|---|---|
| Reading and phonology (*N* = 32) | 7.5 | 5.9 | 93.6 |
| Reading alone (*N* = 31) | 7.5 | 5.9 | 93.1 |
| Phonology alone (*N* = 30) | 7.5 | 5.9 | 94.6 |
| Control (*N* = 31) | 7.6 | 6.0 | 93.2 |

7 year olds because by this age it is possible to identify with some certainty those who are experiencing difficulties in learning to read.

## Baseline assessment

We gave the children their first assessment before the training began. This was in September 1989. They were re-assessed some seven months later, after the intervention was completed. This was in April–May 1990. The twenty weeks of teaching were spread over a twenty-five-week period between mid-October and early April. We were interested to see if any improvements in reading persisted beyond the end of the intervention, so we assessed the children for a third time in January 1991, nine months after the interventions had ceased.

At the beginning of the study, we gave all the children tests measuring their reading, spelling, arithmetic and phonological skills. Including the BAS Word Reading Test,[12] on which children were matched, there were four different measures of reading in our battery of tests. We used the BAS test as a normative measure of context-free word recognition. Normative tests can be insensitive to differences between children at a very early stage of learning to read, so we devised an Early Word Recognition Test to assess progress at the very early stage of acquiring a 'sight vocabulary'. This test required the children to read aloud words that commonly appear in the first books children come across. The Neale Analysis of Reading Ability (revised, Form 1)[13] was used as a measure of reading accuracy in context (i.e. when reading passages of text rather than just single words). The Neale Analysis also measures reading comprehension through questions asked about each passage. We also gave the children a nonword reading test. As we have noted, this type of test provides a relatively pure measure of phonic recoding skill. The test consisted of seventy non-words each of which could be pronounced using standard phonic conventions (e.g. 'um', 'bac', 'blod', 'kond', 'vone', 'fepple' and 'unplint').

The Schonell Graded Word Spelling Test:[14] List B was used to measure spelling ability and the BAS Basic Number Skills Test:[12] Test A was used to measure arithmetic skills. If maths skills had improved as well as reading skills, then it is likely that the training effects would have been of a general nature and not specific to reading and spelling. Children's mean scores on the reading, spelling and arithmetic tests are shown in table 5.2.

We used four measures of phonological processing to monitor the children's development of phonological skills. The measures of phonological processing covered skills that most children can demonstrate before they can read (sound categorization), skills normally acquired at about the age of beginning to read (phoneme blending and segmentation) and skills typically acquired after two or more years of reading experience (phoneme deletion).

A modified version of Lynette Bradley's sound categorization test[15] was used to measure the ability to recognize rhyme and alliteration in spoken words. The test consisted of thirty sets of four words. Within each set, three words contained a common sound that the fourth lacked. The first twenty sets were rhyme oddity tasks, with the distinctive sound being the last consonant in the first ten sets (e.g. which is the odd one out in 'pin, win, sit, fin'?) and the medial vowel in the second ten (e.g. which is the odd one out in 'lot, cot, pot, hat'?). The final ten sets of words constituted an alliteration oddity task (e.g. which is the odd one out in 'ham, tap, had, hat'?).

A Sound Blending Test was constructed and used to measure the ability to blend a sequence of sounds into nonwords. The test stimuli consisted of thirty sets of two to seven sounds (e.g. 'a' 'b', 'r' 'e' 'l', 'h' 'u' 'p' 't' and 'i' 'd' 'o' 'c' 't'). When presenting consonant sounds, the examiner tried to ensure that the vowel following each consonant (e.g. the 'uh' sound after the 'k' in 'k'

*Table 5.2* Means (average scores) for the pre- and post-intervention attainment measures of reading, spelling and arithmetic in the four groups

|  |  | Reading and phonology | Reading alone | Phonology alone | Control |
|---|---|---|---|---|---|
| N |  | 32 | 31 | 30 | 31 |
| Early word | t1 | 20.2 | 20.1 | 21.0 | 0.9 |
| identification[a] | t2 | 32.7 | 32.3 | 29.7 | 29.3 |
| BAS word | t1 | 5.9 | 5.9 | 5.9 | 6.0 |
| reading[b] | t2 | 6.7 | 6.6 | 6.6 | 6.6 |
| Neale | t1 | 5.1 | 5.0 | 5.2 | 5.1 |
| accuracy[b] | t2 | 6.1 | 5.8 | 5.8 | 5.7 |
|  | t3 | 6.8 | 6.2 | 6.3 | 6.3 |
| Neale | t1 | 5.3 | 5.3 | 5.4 | 5.4 |
| comprehension[b] | t2 | 6.4 | 6.0 | 5.9 | 5.9 |
|  | t3 | 7.0 | 6.5 | 6.5 | 6.4 |
| Nonword | t1 | 4.3 | 3.6 | 6.0 | 3.7 |
| reading[c] | t2 | 15.6 | 10.8 | 15.5 | 11.9 |
| Schonell | t1 | 5.8 | 5.8 | 5.9 | 5.8 |
| spelling[b] | t2 | 6.8 | 6.5 | 6.7 | 6.5 |
|  | t3 | 7.2 | 6.9 | 7.0 | 6.9 |
| BAS | t1 | 6.6 | 6.8 | 6.8 | 6.7 |
| arithmetic[b] | t2 | 7.4 | 7.5 | 7.4 | 7.4 |

[a] Maximum score, 42.
[b] Attainment ages expressed in years.
[c] Maximum score, 70.

'i' 'f') was reduced to a minimum. Phonemes can rarely be isolated within words, and there is a tendency for people to emphasize sound in words by pronouncing them as syllables (e.g. 'kuh' 'a' 'tuh'). These are not phonemes.

The nonword segmentation test consisted of thirty sets of nonwords, each consisting of between two and seven phonemes. We required the children to segment the nonwords into separate sounds and to push a coin forward as they spoke each sound. For each item, we gave the children the number of coins corresponding to its constituent sounds.

A modified version of D. J. Bruce's Word Analysis Test[16] was used to measure phoneme deletion (the ability to delete sounds from spoken words). In section one of the test, the sound to be

*Table 5.3*  Means (average scores) for the pre- and post-intervention raw scores on measures of phonological ability for the four groups

|  |  | Reading and phonology | Reading alone | Phonology alone | Control |
|---|---|---|---|---|---|
| N |  | 32 | 31 | 30 | 31 |
| Sound | t1 | 2.9 | 2.9 | 3.8 | 2.4 |
| deletion[a] | t2 | 9.9 | 6.2 | 13.7 | 7.4 |
| Nonword | t1 | 9.3 | 10.3 | 11.4 | 8.3 |
| segmentation[b] | t2 | 15.8 | 16.1 | 18.6 | 14.9 |
| Sound | t1 | 9.6 | 6.0 | 7.6 | 7.1 |
| blending[b] | t2 | 12.1 | 10.7 | 14.4 | 11.0 |
| Sound | t1 | 14.3 | 13.8 | 14.6 | 13.3 |
| categorization[b] | t2 | 17.6 | 16.9 | 18.3 | 15.7 |

[a] Maximum score, 24.
[b] Maximum score, 30.

deleted was the first one in a word. A typical question was 'What word is left if the "j" sound is taken away from the beginning of "jam"?' In sections two and three, the sound to be deleted occurred respectively at the end and in the middle position of words. In section four, the position of the sound to be deleted was varied. Children's mean scores on the phoneme deletion test and the other three measures of phonological awareness are shown in table 5.3.

## General framework for the intervention

The ninety-three children in the three experimental groups were given forty thirty-minute sessions spread over twenty weeks by a total of twenty-three teachers. These were eight learning-support teachers who visited the schools, seven school-based special-needs teachers, seven class teachers and one Headteacher. Each was granted relief from their normal duties in order to receive a three-day training in how to use the materials and to carry out the research interventions.

During the intervention period, each teacher worked individually with between two and nine children. Most of the teachers were involved with sets of three children (one from each experimental group). To avoid children always being taught at the same time, we varied the times of the day that they were taught. We monitored strict adherence to the different teaching procedures via regular meetings with the principal investigator (Peter Hatcher) and through the analysis of written records for each teaching session.

## The teaching Programmes

### Phonological training alone (P)

The phonological training package was written with the support and advice of a speech therapist, an adviser for early childhood education, two learning support teachers, a Headteacher and six teachers with a wide range of primary school teaching experience. The package was purely phonological, involving no reading. It consisted of nine sections of phonological tasks based broadly on the 'levels of difficulty' and activities referred to by researchers such as Lewkowicz[17] (Ohio), Lundberg et al.[3] (Umea, Sweden), Rosner[18] (Pittsburgh), Stanovich et al.[19] (New York) and Yopp[20] (California). The sections covered (a) the identification and supply of rhyming words, (b) the identification of words as units within sentences, (c) the identification and manipulation of syllables, (d) the identification and discrimination of phonemes within words, (e) phoneme blending, (f) phoneme segmentation, (g) phoneme deletion, (h) phoneme substitution and (i) phoneme transposition. Some of the phoneme deletion, blending and segmentation activities were equivalent to those used in the phonological portions of the assessment battery, but involved the use of different materials.

Each section of the phonological training package consisted of a number of activities which varied in terms of mode of presentation (pictures and/or aural), task and level of difficulty. Just as the first section was considered to be the easiest, and the last section the hardest, the activities within each section were ordered from easiest to hardest. For example, activities were ordered according to the position of manipulation within words (initial, final or medial) and according to the number of stimuli that children had to manipulate (two to five).

In a chapter of this nature, it is only possible to present an overview of the programme. We therefore list, below, some of the sets of activities involved in each section. Examples of specific activities are also presented. The complete package of materials (seventy activities, pictures and photocopyable record sheets) is available elsewhere (Hatcher[21]).

(a)  Identification and supply of rhyming words
   (i)    Introduction to rhyme
   (ii)   Discrimination of pairs of rhyming and non-rhyming words
   (iii)  Supplying rhymes
   (iv)   Discrimination of one of three words that rhymes with a target word
(b)  Identification of words as units within sentences
   (i)    Introduction to the concepts 'beginning', 'middle' and 'end'
   (ii)   Comprehension of the concepts 'beginning', 'middle' and 'end' in sentences
   (iii)  Transfer of the concepts of 'beginning', 'middle' and 'end' to aural activities
   (iv)   Production of 'initial', 'final' and 'medial' words in sentences of two to four words
   (v)    Matching counters to words in two- to five-word sentences
(c)  Identification and manipulation of syllables
   (i)    Introduction to syllabic rhythm in poems
   (ii)   Syllable blending
   (iii)  Introduction to syllable segmentation
   (iv)   Segmentation of words into syllables
   (v)    Syllable counting (with counters)
   (vi)   Syllable deletion
(d)  Identification and discrimination of phonemes
   (i)    Introduction to saying a word slowly
   (ii)   Picture–sound association
   (iii)  Word pair discrimination
   (iv)   Identification of initial, final and medial sounds in words
   (v)    Discrimination of two of three words with the same initial, final or medial sound

    (vi)  Discrimination of one of three words with the same initial or final sound as a target word

(e)  Phoneme blending

    (i–v)  Production of words from two to five (phoneme) sounds

(f)  Phoneme segmentation

    (i)  Production of the initial, final or medial sound of target words

    (ii)  Introduction to the concept of 'breaking up a word' into sounds

    (iii)  Introduction to segmenting a word while simultaneously putting counters into boxes

    (iv)  Phoneme counting (with counters)

    (v)  Segmenting words into sounds (without counters)

(g)  Phoneme deletion

    (i)  Introduction to the concepts of 'take away' and 'left' in relation to sounds in words

    (ii)  Specification of initial, final or medial sounds deleted from words

    (iii)  Deletion of the initial, final or medial sound from words to produce different words

(h)  Phoneme substitution

    (i)  Introduction to the concept of changing the beginning item of a sequence

    (ii)  Revision of the concept of 'first sound in a word'

    (iii)  Changing the initial sound of a word

    (iv)  Substituting initial, final or medial sounds in words

(i)  Phoneme transposition

    (i)  Defining the concept of 'backwards'

    (ii)  Reversing the sequence of sounds in words

    (iii)  Introduction to Spoonerisms

    (iv)  Spoonerisms

The teachers presented the activities to children as sequenced in the package and at a rate commensurate with their success with the materials. Apart from activities where concepts were being explained, each activity began with three teaching examples. These were followed by a set of six screening items. If children were credited with 100 per cent success on these (without any teacher help), they were moved on to the next activity. Otherwise, the 'missed' items were used as teaching points and a further twelve items were presented to children. If children were credited with at least ten correct responses for the twelve items (80 per cent success criteria) they progressed to the next activity. Otherwise, teachers gave them more practice with similar items (constructed by themselves), used parallel game-like activities from an appendix of additional activities, or reverted to a lower level in the package. After that, teachers were instructed to move children on to the next activity rather than persisting with a task that was particularly difficult. Progression from one section to another was also determined by the 80 per cent success criteria. In this case, children should have been successful with at least 80 per cent of the activities in a section.

As an example of an activity in section (a) 'Identification and supply of rhyming words', we present a description of a task where children had to discriminate one of three words that rhymed with a target word. Teachers introduced the task by saying 'I am going to say a word and I want you to listen to it carefully . . . "House". Now listen to these words and choose one that rhymes with house: Monkey . . . Dog . . . Mouse.' Two further teaching examples were given like this (Minder: Castle . . . Finder . . . Table; Monday: Sunday . . . Cabbage . . . Butter). If children got the next six items right, teachers concluded that they could do the task and moved them on to the next activity. Otherwise, as indicated above, the 'missed' items were used as teaching points and a further twelve items were presented to them.

Following a similar format, a phoneme counting (with counters) activity, from section (f) 'Phoneme segmentation', required children to segment words into phonemes using picture sheets, counters and a board with six boxes marked on it. Teachers were instructed to say 'Here is a picture of/for . . . (name the object/ concept). You say it. Now I want you to break up the words into sounds. As you say each sound put a marker on the board.' The three practice items ('in', 'pin'; 'sea', 'seat'; 'lock' and 'clock') were presented as pairs of words in order to enhance attention to the differences (a single phoneme) between similar sounding words. Since pairs of words were used throughout this activity, the screening items involved six pairs of words and the remaining items consisted of twelve pairs of words.

One of the activities, from section (g) 'Phoneme deletion', required children to delete the initial sound of a word to produce another word. The instructions given to them were 'Listen to the word . . . "farm" . . . You say it. If you take away the "f" sound, what word is left?' The practice examples were 'farm' (arm), 'pair' (air) and 'spot' (pot). Again, there were six screening items and twelve further items.

As noted above, additional activities, listed in an appendix to the programme, were used to help children master section objectives. They were also used as easy to hard fun-activities. For example, under section (c) 'Identification and manipulation of syllables', the easiest activity required teachers and children to make a list of about twenty one- to four-syllable spoken words known to the children. The children were then required to clap the parts they could hear in the one- and two-syllable words. They progressed to three- and four-syllable words as appropriate. The hardest fun-activity in section (c) involved teachers and children playing aural dominoes. Each player had to supply two words. The first word had to contain the same number of syllables as the last word supplied by the other player. The second word could contain any number of syllables. In practice, teachers found that children worked best if the sessions were broken into three parts, with the middle part being spent on these 'fun'-activities.

## Reading with phonology (R + P)

The reading with phonology training package was written with the support and advice of the same people who helped produce the phonological training package. It was modelled on Marie Clay's[22] early intervention procedures, and included additional phonological activities. Some of these were to be completed on their own: others were to be explicitly linked with reading and writing.

## Initial assessment of children's strengths and weaknesses

The first four of the forty thirty-minute R + P sessions were taken up by teachers assessing children's responses to easy to hard text, words and letters. The teachers gave the children a number of tests, assessing their concepts about print; their ability to identify and write letters; their ability to write a story and read it back; the quality of their handwriting; their level of written language; their punctuation; and their reading and writing vocabulary. In addition, children were assessed as to their ability to perceive words as units within a spoken message, to articulate words slowly, to break up unknown words into sounds, and to write consonants or vowels of unknown words using sound analysis.

Children's verbal responses when reading 100 to 200 words of text were recorded on a blank piece of paper using a coding system and analysed with respect to reading accuracy, level of text (easy, instructional or hard), self-correction rates and the incidence of self-help and teacher-related behaviours. The children's reading behaviour was also analysed in terms of their responses to text, words and letters. The text reading behaviours examined included directional movement, errors (based on meaning, grammar or the appearance of words), self-correction behaviour, and the degree of cross-checking of semantic, grammatical, visual and letter-sound clues. As well as being part of the assessment battery, Clay's 'Running Record' was an integral part of each teaching session.

A link was made between the diagnostic tests and fifteen sets of teaching strategies via summary record and strategy sheets. The summary strategy sheet allowed teachers to make brief notes from the various record sheets under the headings text, word and letter strategies, and following the dichotomy of reading strengths and weaknesses. The teachers were then referred to a chart which linked identified areas of weakness to specific teaching strategies. For example, if a child was perceived to have difficulty in acquiring an early reading vocabulary teachers were directed to the set of strategies under the headings 'Learning to look at print (words)', 'Writing stories' and 'When it is hard to remember'. If a child was perceived to have difficulty in using letters and sounds to read and write, teachers were directed to the sections on 'Hearing sounds in words and teaching for word analysis' and 'Linking sound and letter sequence.'

## Teaching activities

The fifteen sets of teaching strategies covered the directional rules of print, one-to-one correspondence of spoken and written words, the ability to recognize and write letters and words, the ability to write a story and to establish sound–symbol relationships, the ability to be flexible in the use of spacing within and between words, and the abilities to self-monitor reading, search for and cross-check semantic, grammatical, visual and letter–sound clues, self-correct reading errors and to read with phrasing and fluency. Common to the teaching strategies were the general principles of reviewing previous learning, setting small, sequential learning steps from the known to the new, modelling desired behaviour followed by prompting and fading of prompts, praising closer approximations towards goals, requiring the generalization of new skills to other mediums or settings, providing overlearning experiences, preventing errors and confusion from arising, and avoiding unnecessary frustration.

One of the strategies for remembering words included attaching a small visual symbol to one of its letters in representation of the child's perception of its meaning, then later fading the visual clue. For example, if a child associated the word 'man' with his dad wearing a hat, the teacher might draw a small hat over the word 'man'. Over time the symbol would gradually be rubbed out or 'faded'. Other strategies included the multisensory approaches described by Marie Clay[22] and by Peter Bryant and Lynette Bradley.[23] Clay's procedure of 'trace and say, imagine and say, look and say, and write and say' draws children's attention to the overall appearance of words. Bryant and Bradley's approach of 'look and say, write and say the letter names, and look and say' draws children's attention to words being formed of sequences of distinct letters.

When reading books, children were encouraged to integrate the use of their existing skills. The 'reading books' strategies included the teacher introducing the plot of a story (at the instructional level) and drawing attention to unusual language, children reading on their own and being given support when difficulties were met, children and teachers reading together to encourage fluency, and teachers taking a running record of children reading and drawing attention to text or word cues when errors had been recorded. The books used by the children were selected mainly from the series 'Story Chest' (Arnold Wheaton), 'Oxford Reading Tree' (Oxford University Press), 'Shorty' books (Ginn) and 'Monster' books (Longman). The sequence of the books, according to the New Zealand Department of Education's 1987[24] classification of children's reading books, corresponded closely with the publishers' ordering of them. Approximately three to four books were provided at each of the twenty levels of text difficulty.

Only two of the groups of activities described by Clay[22] were changed significantly. These were 'Hearing sounds in words' and 'Teaching for word analysis'. These sets of activities were synthesized and the section ordered and extended to include additional phonological linkage activities and references to the rhyming, word, syllable and phoneme activities from the phonological training package. The purpose of this set of activities was to encourage children to hear sounds in words and to make the link between sounds and the written form of words. With regard to the latter, children were encouraged to segment new words into sounds prior to writing them, using Elkonin's[25] technique, and to identify specific sounds in phonemically simple words using plastic letters, following Bradley's (Bryant and Bradley[23]) technique. The use of plastic letters was also extended to words containing consonant blends (e.g. 'nt' in went, pant and pint) and digraphs (e.g. 'ai' in rain, pain and mail). Wherever possible, all of these activities were related to words derived from children's reading and writing.

## The format of the teaching sessions

Each of sessions 5 to 40 followed the format:

1  Re-reading a book that could be read with greater than 94 per cent accuracy (easy level).
2  Reading the book introduced at the end of the previous session with teachers taking a running record of children's responses

to 100–200 words. If the book was read with 90–94 per cent accuracy (instructional level) then teachers introduced another book from the same level at the end of the session. Where children read books fluently with greater than 94 per cent accuracy during two to three consecutive sessions, teachers introduced a book at a higher level at the end of the session.

3 Identifying letters (where necessary).
4 Phonological training activities.
5 Writing a story (including 'Hearing sounds in words' and 'Teaching for word analysis').
6 Cutting up the story (where necessary).
7 Being introduced to a new book
8 Attempting to read the new book, with teacher encouragement of independent reading, and then with shared reading.

After each session, the teachers made a record of the content of the session in order to monitor children's progress and plan for future lessons. Reading progression therefore followed a cycle of

1 consolidating children's reading strengths with material that could be read with more than 94 per cent accuracy (independent level);
2 working to overcome confusions and learning new skills with text that could be read with 90–94 per cent accuracy (instructional level);
3 identifying the set of skills to be taught at the next level through a running record of children's responses to text at that level, as well as through their writing and phonological linkage activities.

## Reading alone (R)

The reading alone package was identical to that used with the R + P group except for the omission of any explicit reference to phonology and all of the teaching strategies concerned with phonological linkage activities. In the early stages of the intervention period, teachers were frequently reminded of the importance of not referring to phonology or letter–sound relationships. Where children already exhibited such skills, teachers accepted demonstrations of that knowledge but made neither positive nor negative comments about them. In place of the explicit phonological linkage instruction given to the R + P group, group R spent more time building up reading and writing vocabularies through the use of multisensory teaching techniques, learning the names of letters and reading books. Their reading instruction involved more time on the usefulness of context and meaning in reading, and on the use of self-checking and correction for attempts at reading unknown words. In short, the programme involved the same degree of individualized, highly structured, teaching as the R + P programme but it lacked the explicit phonological and phonological linkage instruction given to the R + P group.

## *Control (C)*

The children in this group received their regular classroom teaching without any additional input from our study. Some of the children in the group, like those in the other groups, received additional remedial teaching that was independent of that provided by our study. However, the number of such children in the control group (fifteen) was greater than the numbers in the other groups (R + P, 5; R, 7, and P, 6). It should also be noted that virtually all the children in the study received some phonic reading instruction at school. However, this provision did not involve exercises in phonological awareness of the sort used with the P and R + P groups.

## **Results**

The aim of our study was to test the relative effectiveness of three teaching methods in helping children who were experiencing difficulties in the early stages of learning to read. We were therefore interested in the relative progress of the groups in learning to read and spell between the first and second assessments (i.e. over the period of the intervention).

All four groups, including the unseen control group, made progress from the first to the second assessment, but this is only to be expected given that twenty-five weeks of normal schooling elapsed for all of the children between the two assessments. What matters is whether any of the experimental intervention groups improved *more* than the control children on any of the tests. Table 5.2 shows that the R + P group consistently made the largest improvements in reading and spelling. The R + P group made significantly more progress than the control group on every single measure of literacy. Although the scores of the R and P groups at the second assessment tended to be ahead of those of the controls, these differences were not large or consistent enough to be statistically significant. The sole exception to this was the Early Word Recognition Test where the R group made more progress than the control group.

Changes in mathematical skills were similar in all four groups, with the three treatment groups failing to make faster progress than the control group. This indicates that the treatment effects found for reading and spelling were specific to those skills, and were not due to any general factor such as motivation or increases in teachers' expectations.

For most of the tests the results are presented as attainment ages. Thus, if we consider the performance of the R + P group on the accuracy measure of the Neale Analysis of Reading Ability,[13] we can see that at the first assessment, before the intervention began, these $7\frac{1}{2}$-year-old poor readers were performing at a level that we would expect to see in normal readers aged just over 5 years. By the time of the second assessment, following twenty weeks of intervention, they had gained a whole year in reading age, advancing from 5.1 to 6.1 At the third assessment, after nine months with no special treatment, their reading accuracy was equivalent to that of normal 6.8 year olds. By now they were about 9 years old, so their reading was still below what one might ideally like to see, but it was still ahead of the control group who had received no special treatment and whose reading ages on the Neale accuracy measure rose from 5.1 at the outset of the study to 5.7 at the second assessment and 6.3 at the third.

The method of statistical analysis that we adopted allowed us to contrast the scores of each of the three experimental groups at the second assessment with those of the control group, while accounting for any differences between the literacy scores of the groups at the time of the first assessment. Prior to completing the analyses, and in line with the requirements of the tests used, we excluded the results for one child. (Readers interested in the details of how the results were analysed are referred to our original paper[2] published in the journal *Child Development*.)

In order to determine the extent to which the differential effects of the teaching programmes were maintained, we assessed the children's reading and spelling attainments nine months after the intervention had ceased. The children's scores on the Neale Analysis[13] and Schonell[14] tests at that point are shown in table 5.2. Statistical analyses confirmed that the R + P group had maintained its advantage over the control group even nine months after the intervention had finished. As before, neither the R group nor the P group differed significantly from the control group. The results with spelling were more disappointing, with none of the treatment groups differing significantly from the control group at the nine-month reassessment.

Our phonological linkage hypothesis holds that, in order to be effective in increasing reading skills, the training of phonological and reading skills needs to be integrated. The results strongly support this position. Working away at phonological analysis without reference to reading and writing is of no help to poor readers. Similarly, and perhaps more controversially, working away at reading skills with no reference to phonics is equally unhelpful. The benefits of integrated reading plus phonology training were not of a general nature, but were specific to reading and spelling, and the reading gains, at least, were durable.

Analysis of performance on the purely phonological tests in our battery (sound categorization, blending, deletion etc.) showed that only group P improved more than the control group, yet that improvement in phonological awareness did not carry over into reading and writing (because, we would argue, the children were not taught how to *apply* their improved understanding of sound structure to the business of reading and writing). The results also indicate that it is relatively difficult to improve the phonological skills of poor readers. Although group R + P spent a considerable amount of time being trained on phonological tasks, it was not enough to bring about a significant improvement in their phonological skills.

## Implications of the Results

In line with the phonological linkage hypothesis, our study shows that a combined phonological–literacy skills training approach is effective in boosting the reading skills of reading-delayed 7-year-olds. Spending an equivalent amount of time on phonology alone or on reading without phonology is of little or no use. These results are particularly striking when one considers that the children in the R + P group spent less time on reading activities than did the children in the R group.

The R + P programme was modelled on Marie Clay's[22] approach, though it did not follow her programme slavishly. Although Clay's reading recovery programme is of proven effectiveness, we doubt that anyone would claim that it represents the last word in reading intervention for poor readers. Recently, Sandra Iversen and William Tunmer[26] in the State of Rhode Island compared the effectiveness of an unchanged Clay reading recovery programme with that of a modified programme in which children received more systematic phonological training. The modified programme proved to be 37 per cent more effective than the original reading recovery programme, just as our phonological linkage hypothesis would lead us to expect.

An argument that might be levelled against the phonological linkage hypothesis is that explicit linkage activities are not essential: all that is needed is to provide children with both reading and phonological training and they will make the connection for themselves. The results of Byrne and Fielding-Barnsley's[8] study mentioned in the introduction would suggest that this is not the case. Those investigators found that in order for children to understand that particular phonemes in words are matched by particular letters it is necessary for three components to be in place. These are (1) that children can isolate phonemes within words, (2) that they appreciate that sounds can be common between words and (3) that they appreciate that specific sounds can be represented by particular letters. The first two components alone were not enough. Byrne and Fielding-Barnsley found that the children in their study needed to be explicitly taught to make the connection between letters and sounds within words.

Contrary to what one might have expected, group P did not make greater progress in learning to spell than the control group. Usha Goswami and Peter Bryant,[27] and Margaret Snowling and Charles Hulme,[28] have argued that reading and spelling develop partially independently and that phonological strategies are more important for the development of early spelling than early reading. Given that the phonological programme did not bring about an improvement in spelling greater than that seen in the control children, and that the R + P programme did, our results do not support this position. Instead they argue for an association between the development of reading and writing skills, and that for children having difficulties in the early stages of learning to read and spell, a combined programme of reading, writing and phonological training can be expected to improve both their reading and spelling.

From an educational point of view, the results are in line with the consistent findings, reviewed by Jeanne Chall[29] and more recently by Marilyn Adams,[30] that phonic-based methods are more effective than visual teaching methods. However, it must be stressed that the R + P programme did not constitute an out-of-context, phonics-based approach. It required children to *integrate* the use of phonological, visual, semantic and syntactic strategies.

It is inevitable that some issues remain unresolved. One is the extent to which the intervention which we have found effective for 7-year-old poor readers would work for other age and ability groups. Given Iversen and Tunmer's[26] findings with reading-delayed 6-year-old children, there would appear to be little reason to believe that the effects would not generalize to younger children with reading difficulties, but only by systematically evaluating the effectiveness of different interventions with different groups of readers will we discover how far these findings can be extended.

A related issue is whether all poor readers are capable of benefiting from integrated reading-with-phonology training. Many children of high IQ with specific reading difficulties experience profound phonological difficulties (see the review by Charles

Hulme and Margaret Snowling[31]). It is possible that some children with very severe phonological problems might be immune to the effects of phonological training. Examples of such cases are discussed in several papers written by Margaret Snowling[32] and her colleagues Charles Hulme[33] and Joy Stackhouse.[34] There were three children in our study who exhibited very poor phonological processing skills at the first assessment and who made little progress with reading and spelling over the period of the intervention. By chance, these three children were all in the R + P group. The implication is that a minority of poor readers may struggle to benefit from an integrated reading-with-phonology package. (Whether they would benefit more from any other sort of intervention is an open question.) The consolation is that the progress of the R + P group looks even more dramatic with these three children taken out. Even with them in, though, the improvements of the R + P group over the course of the intervention are impressive. Over a period of about six months (twenty weeks with two half-hour sessions per week, plus holidays), their reading ages on the Neale test improved by over a year in terms of both accuracy and comprehension. The control group came on by less than six months of reading age (because poor readers make slow progress, and tend as a result to fall further and further behind their classmates). Hence the R + P group improved more than twice as quickly as would otherwise have been expected – on the basis of just two half-hours per week.

The scores at the nine-month follow-up suggest that the reading performance of the R + P group, though still ahead of that of the controls, was tending to fall back again. Ted Glynn and his colleagues T. Crooks, N. Bethune, K. Ballard and J. Smith[35] have pointed to a similar effect with reading recovery in New Zealand. Bill Tunmer[36] has argued that the reading recovery programme pays too little attention to phonological awareness and to letter – sound relationships, and without that element its effectiveness fades. Although the R + P programme specifically included activities of this nature, it is possible that some of the children in our study needed more than the forty thirty-minute teaching sessions they received. It is also possible they may have continued to benefit from the programme had it been integrated with the provision made by their schools. Clay[21] argues that her teaching procedures need to form part of a total system of provision involving the children, their parents, their teachers, and the educational system at the school and regional levels. These are issues for future studies to address. Additional well designed, properly controlled and appropriately analysed studies are badly needed if we are to take the teaching of reading out of the realms of fad and fashion and place it on a firm, rational, empirical footing.

## NOTES

1   Bradley, L. and Bryant, P.E. 1983: 'Categorising sounds and learning to read: a causal connexion', *Nature*, 301, 419–21.
2   Hatcher, P.J., Hulme, C. and Ellis, A.W. 1994: 'Ameliorating early reading failure by integrating the teaching of reading and phonological skills: the phonological linkage hypothesis', *Child Development*, 65, 41–5.
3   Lundberg, I., Frost, J. and Peterson, O. 1988: 'Effects of an extensive program for stimulating phonological awareness in pre-school children', *Reading Research Quarterly* 23, 263–84.
4   Cunningham, A.E. 1990: 'Explicit versus implicit instruction in phonemic awareness', *Journal of Experimental Child Psychology*, 50, 429–44.
5   Ball, E.W. and Blachman, B.A. 1988: 'Phoneme segmentation training: éffect on reading readiness', *Annals of Dyslexia*, 38, 208–25.
6   Ball, E.W. and Blachman, B.A. 1991: 'Does phoneme awareness training in kindergarten make a difference in early word recognition and developmental spelling?', *Reading Research Quarterly*, 26, 49–66.
7   Tunmer, W.E., Herriman, M.L. and Nesdale, A.R. 1988: 'Metalinguistic awareness abilities and beginning reading', *Reading Research Quarterly*, 23 134–58.
8   Byrne, B. and Fielding-Barnsley, R. 1989: 'Phonemic awareness and letter knowledge in the child's acquisition of the alphabetic principle', *Journal of Educational Psychology*, 81, 313–21.
9   Carver, C. 1970: *Word Recognition Test*, London: Hodder and Stoughton.
10  Raven, J.C. 1965: *The Coloured Progressive Matrices Test*, London: Lewis.
11  Wechsler, D. 1974: *Wechsler Intelligence Scale for Children – Revised*, New York: Psychological Corporation.
12  Elliott, C.D., Murray, D.J. and Pearson, L.S. 1983: *British Ability Scales*, Windsor: NFER-Nelson.
13  Neale, M.D. 1989: *Neale Analysis of Reading Ability*, revised British edn, Windsor: NFER-Nelson.
14  Schonell, F.J. and Schonell, F.E. 1956: *Diagnostic and Attainment Testing: Including a Manual of Tests, their Nature, Use, Recording and Interpretation*, London: Oliver and Boyd.

15  Bradley, L. 1984: *Assessing Reading Difficulties: A Diagnostic and Remedial Approach*, 2nd edn, London: Macmillan Educational.
16  Bruce, D.J. 1964: 'The analysis of word sounds by young children', *British Journal of Educational Psychology*, 34, 158–70.
17  Lewkowicz, N.K. 1980: 'Phonemic awareness training: what to teach and how to teach it', *Journal of Educational Psychology*, 72, 686–700.
18  Rosner, J. 1975: *Helping Children Overcome Learning Difficulties: A Step-by-step Guide for Parents and Teachers*, New York: Walker.
19  Stanovich, K.E., Cunningham, A.E. and Cramer, B.B. 1984: 'Assessing phonological skills in kindergarten children: issues of task comparability', *Journal of Experimental Child Psychology*, 38, 175–90.
20  Yopp, H.K. 1988: 'The validity and reliability of phonemic awareness tests', *Reading Research Quarterly*, 23 159–77.
21  Hatcher, P.J. 1994: *Sound Linkage: An Integrated Programme for Overcoming Reading Difficulties*, London: Whurr.
22  Clay, M. 1985: *The Early Detection of Reading Difficulties*, 3rd edn, Tadworth, Surrey: Heinemann.
23  Bryant, P.E. and Bradley, L. 1985: *Children's Reading Difficulties*, Oxford: Blackwell.
24  New Zealand Department of Education 1987: *Classified Guide of Complementary Reading Materials – Books for Junior Classes: A Classified Guide for Teachers*, Wellington: Department of Education.
25  Elkonin, D.B. 1973: 'USSR', in J. Downing (ed.), *Comparitive Reading: Cross National Studies of Behaviour and Processes in Reading and Writing*, London: Collier-Macmillan.
26  Iversen, S. and Tunmer, W.E. 1993: 'Phonological processing and the reading recovery program', *Journal of Educational Psychology*, 85, 112–26.
27  Goswami, U. and Bryant, P. 1990: *Phonological Skills and Learning to Read*, London: Lawrence Erlbaum.
28  Snowling, M. and Hulme, C. 1991: 'Speech processing and learning to spell', in R. Ellis and R. Bowler (eds), *Language and the Creation of Literacy*, Baltimore, M.D: Orton Dyslexia Society, 33–9.
29  Chall, J.S. 1983: *Learning to Read: The Great Debate*, 2nd edn, New York: McGraw-Hill.
30  Adams, M.J. 1990: *Beginning to Read: Learning and Thinking About Print*, Cambridge, MA: MIT Press.
31  Hulme, C. and Snowling, M. 1991: 'Phonological deficits in dyslexia: a "sound" reappraisal of the verbal deficit hypothesis?', in N. Singh and I. Beale (eds), *Progress in Learning Disabilities*, New York: Springer, 260–83.
32  Snowling, M. and Hulme, C. 1989: 'A longitudinal case study of developmental phonological dyslexia', *Cognitive Neuropsychology*, 6 379–401.
33  Hulme, C. and Snowling, M. 1992: 'Deficits in output phonology: a cause of reading failure?', *Cognitive Neuropsychology*, 9, 47–72.
34  Stackhouse, J. and Snowling, M. 1992: 'Barriers to literacy development in two cases of developmental verbal dyspraxia', *Cognitive Neuropsychology*, 9 273–99.

35 Glynn, T., Crooks, T., Bethune, N., Ballard, K. and Smith, J. 1989: *Reading Recovery in Context*, Wellington: Department of Education.
36 Tunmer, W.E. 1992: 'Phonological processing and reading recovery: a reply to Clay', *New Zealand Journal of Educational Studies*, 27, 203–17.

# 6

# Learning to Understand Written Language

## Jane Oakhill and Nicola Yuill

*We read to gain information and to be entertained. Reading is therefore about understanding, not word recognition.*

*We have concentrated so far in this book on word recognition skills, since these are the skills which beginner readers need to obtain before they can begin to understand what they read. However, it cannot be assumed that once children have acquired word recognition and word decoding skills they will then become good readers. Some children appear to decode written words more successfully than they understand them. At its most extreme, occasional children and adults are reported who are able to read aloud irregular words and novel words, and yet are unable to understand the individual words they can read. Such cases are referred to as 'hyperlexia', and are associated with very low IQ.*

*In this chapter Jane Oakhill and Nicola Yuill discuss the case of children who, unlike hyperlexic children, fall within the normal IQ range and yet nevertheless fail to comprehend fully what they read. The meanings of individual words are not the problem; rather, the difficulty lies in understanding the content of what they read: the structure and point of a story and the inferences necessary to understand points not explicitly made. What is more, investigations conducted by the authors have shown that the problem is not confined to understanding written text, but is apparent in other language-based tasks too, and can even be observed in children's own attempts to structure a story when describing events in a series of pictures. Clearly understanding and recognizing these different levels of language comprehension in children is of vital importance to the teacher and child in the classroom.*

*Encouragingly, preliminary attempts at remedial teaching of comprehension skills of poor comprehenders have been successful, at least over the short term, suggesting that some children may not have been exposed to narrative sufficiently often to develop these skills unaided. On the basis of further evidence, the authors tentatively propose that reading aloud to children may be one way to develop these skills naturally at an early age.*

## Introduction

In this chapter, we will be considering the problems of children who have good word recognition, can understand sentences and can read aloud apparently fluently, but who have only a rudimentary understanding of what they have just read. There are many skills needed to understand a text adequately. The meanings of the individual sentences and paragraphs must be integrated, and the main ideas of the text identified. On-going comprehension also needs to be monitored, so that any failures can be corrected. We are going to concentrate on three main areas of comprehension skill, and illustrate the problems of less-skilled comprehenders with some of our own work in each of the areas.

The first area is *Inference skills*. In many cases, inferences will be needed to go beyond what is explicitly stated in a text. Authors, of necessity, leave some of the links in a text implicit, and the reader will need to assess, at some level, which inferences need to be made. Second, readers need to *understand the structure* of the text they are reading. In the case of stories, this might include identifying the main character(s) and their motives, following the plot of the story, identifying the main theme. The third area, *comprehension monitoring*, requires the readers to assess their understanding as they are reading. Not only should they be able to identify any comprehension problems, they should know what to do about them, if they do find them. We shall present some of our own research on children with specific comprehension difficulties and, in particular, work that relates to the three areas outlined above.

*Table 6.1* Characteristics of groups of skilled and less-skilled comprehenders

|  | Chronological age (years) | Accuracy age (years) | Comprehension age (years) | Gates–MacGinitie (score/48) |
|---|---|---|---|---|
| Less skilled | 7.9 | 8.4 | 7.3 | 38.0 |
| Skilled | 7.9 | 8.4 | 9.1 | 38.3 |

Our studies have compared groups of skilled and less-skilled comprehenders. Typical groups of subjects are shown in table 6.1.

The groups were selected using the Neale Analysis of Reading Ability and the Gates–NacGinitie Vocabulary Test. The Neale Analysis provides measures both of reading accuracy (word recognition) and comprehension (assessed by ability to answer a series of questions about each passage). The Gates–MacGinitie test requires the child to select one of four words to go with a picture. Thus, it acts as a measure of silent word recognition, and provides an index of the child's vocabulary. In all our studies, the groups of skilled and less-skilled comprehenders were matched for word recognition ability (Neale accuracy and Gates–MacGinitie) and chronological age, but differed in Neale comprehension scores. In general, all children were above average at word recognition. One group were also very good comprehenders; the other group were poor comprehenders, particularly with respect to their ability to recognize words.

Some theories of poor comprehension, for example that of Perfetti,[1] have proposed that comprehension problems are really an extension of word recognition problems. Such theorists argue that accuracy of word recognition is not sufficient for good comprehension: recognition must also be fast and automatic so that, in a limited-capacity system, the lower-level (word recognition) processes do not use up the resources needed for higher-level (comprehension) processes. However, we have found no differences between groups as selected above in decoding speed or automaticity (see Yuill and Oakhill[2]) so, although we do not deny that such factors are likely to lead to comprehension problems in some children, we argue that poor comprehenders exist who do not have difficulties at the word level. Another possibility is that poor comprehenders have difficulties at the level of sentences, failing to understand certain syntactic constructions. However, when we tested the children on Dorothy Bishop's *Test for Reception of Grammar*[3] we found no differences between the groups. Let us turn now to the areas in which we have found differences.

## Making Inferences

One persistent finding in our work is that less-skilled comprehenders have difficulties in making inferences from text. Here, we will outline just one experiment to illustrate the sorts of difficulties that they have. In this experiment, Oakhill[4] explored the children's ability to make inferences about things that were only implicit in texts. The experiment also looked at how the groups responded to the memory demands needed for answering questions about texts. Most measures of comprehension, including the Neale Analysis, require children to answer questions from memory without referring to the text, so one simple, and not very theoretically interesting, explanation of poor comprehenders' problems is that they have a general memory deficit.

To test this possibility, the children were required to answer questions in two conditions: either without referring to the text, or when the text was freely available for them to refer to. They read the passages aloud (and were given help with words as needed) and were then asked two sorts of questions about the text: ones that could be answered from information immediately available in the text (literal), and ones that required an inference. An example text, with questions, is shown below.

### Example story: 'John's Big Test'
John had got up early to learn his spellings. He was very tired and decided to take a break. When he opened his eyes again the first thing he noticed was the clock on the chair. It was an hour later and nearly time for school. He picked up his two books and put them in a bag. He started pedalling to school as fast as he could. However, John ran over some broken bottles and had to walk the rest of the way. By the

*Table 6.2*  Percentages of errors on literal and inferential questions

|  | Unseen | | Seen | |
|  | Literal | Inferential | Literal | Inferential |
| --- | --- | --- | --- | --- |
| Less skilled | 29.2 | 45.8 | 3.6 | 35.4 |
| Skilled | 10.9 | 15.6 | 1.0 | 9.9 |

time he had crossed the bridge and arrived at class, the test was over.

LITERAL QUESTIONS (examples)
1  What was John trying to learn?
2  How many books did John pick up?

INFERENCE QUESTIONS
1  How did John travel to school?
2  What did John do when he decided to take a break?

The child first attempted to answer the questions from memory, and then the experimenter re-presented the questions and asked the child to check the answers to the questions in the text. In this second condition, the child was free to re-read the text to find the answers to the questions. The children's responses to the questions indicated that, as expected, it was easier to answer them with, than without, the text and good comprehenders performed better overall. What was of particular interest, however, were the different patterns of performance between the good and poor comprehenders with and without the passage. The performance of the two groups in the different conditions is shown in table 6.2. When they could not see the passage, the good comprehenders were reasonably good, and better than the less-skilled comprehenders, on both types of question. When the passage was present, the poor comprehenders improved their performance on the literal questions to the same level as that of the good comprehenders in that condition (i.e. near perfect); however, they still made many errors on the questions requiring an inference: over 35 per cent in this condition (the good comprehenders' error rate was 10 per cent). This strikingly high error rate shows that the poor comprehenders' difficulties cannot be attributed to a straightforward memory problem – they have great difficulty in making inferences even with the story available to refer to.

Why might poor comprehenders have such problems? One possibility is that they simply lack the knowledge required to make some of the inferences. We did not test for this possibility explicitly, though it seems likely that 7 year olds would have available such knowledge as that pedalling implies riding a bicycle. Moreover, some recent (unpublished) work by Kate Cain at Sussex has shown that even poor comprehenders do have such knowledge available to them when they are questioned about it directly. A second possibility is that less-skilled comprehenders may not realize the relevance of inferences to understanding a text – they may be concentrating on 'getting the words right', and may process the text at a superficial level. A third possibility is that the children may know about the importance of inferences for text understanding but may be unable to elicit the relevant knowledge and integrate it with the information in the text itself because of processing limitations. We shall argue later that both the second and the third possibilities apply to some extent.

In our book,[2] we review more work showing that less-skilled comprehenders have difficulties with other types of inference. They are less likely to make inferences to connect up ideas from different parts of a text (even when all the information needed for the inferences is explicitly stated in the text), and they are less likely to make inferences about the particular meanings of words from the contexts in which they occur.

## Understanding Text Structure

Our research in this area serves to illustrate the generality of the less-skilled comprehenders' problem, as well as their difficulties in understanding a story's structure. Our main work on children's understanding of story structure comes from tasks where the children were asked to *tell* stories, rather than to read them. Their story-telling was prompted by picture sequences which told a simple story. These experiments showed that less-skilled comprehenders did not seem to have an integrated idea of the stories

*Figure 6.1*　The pictures used in the story retelling experiment

as a whole – they tended to give picture-by-picture accounts rather than connecting together the events in each picture to create a cohesive whole.

One index of story cohesion is the use of connective words, including temporal ones (e.g. *then*), contrastive ones (e.g. *but*) and the most sophisticated ones, causal connectives (e.g. *because*). We told children in the two skill groups a very simple story, with pictures (shown in figure 6.1) containing only temporal connectives (*and, then, when*). Twelve of the sixteen skilled comprehenders, when they retold the story, added new connective terms of all three types, whereas only four of the less-skilled group did so, and none of these additions were causal. The different flavour of the resulting stories is best shown by examples, the first from Anne, a poor comprehender, and the second from Hayley, a good one. The connectives that were not in the original story are in italics.

(ANNE) Sally was getting up for school. Her mum done her lunch-box. She went to school. She's singing a song. She put her lunchbox down. She's doing her lessons. She's doing her lessons again. She goes and gets the wrong lunchbox. She eats the wrong lunch. Another girl came with hers and they had their lunch together.

(HAYLEY) One day there was a little girl and she got off . . . out of bed *because* she . . . she forgot school. [Here the child seemed to mean that the girl was rushing because she had forgotten it was time for school.] Her mum has got . . . has got her breakfast ready. And then she took her lunchbox and said goodbye to her mum. Then she went to school with her lunchbox la'ing to herself. Then she put her lunchbox on the table and then she did her lessons. *After that*, she . . . it was lunchtime, she went to get her lunchbox. *But* she got the wrong lunchbox. *So* they went into the room with different lunchboxes. And then she sat down and she said, 'I've got the wrong sandwiches'. Then she went . . . and another girl came along and said, 'You've got my lunchbox'. *So* they had lunch together. Yum!

Notice that Hayley's story is full of false starts and speech repairs, but shows an obvious attempt to add cohesion to a simple story. Anne's story, on the other hand, is list-like. This impression of a list is created by several features of the story in addition to the lack of connectives. First, Anne uses the present continuous tense (*was getting up, is doing*), which gives a 'running commentary' style, while Hayley uses the past. Anne also repeatedly mentions the same event, and this does not contribute to the story line (*she's doing her lessons again*). This phrase also suggests that she is not recounting a story, but describing in turn the contents of each picture as a separate entity. Hayley's production integrates narrative and descriptive information (*she went to school . . . la'ing to herself*), uses various connectives (e.g. *but, so*), and includes phrases conventionally used in stories (*one day there was . . .*).

This evidence, however, is somewhat impressionistic. We

therefore looked more systematically at children's narrative productions by asking them to tell their own stories from a series of pictures, and we scored their stories for various features that we found to differentiate between the two stories above. First we looked at the tenses of the verbs used. There was a striking difference between the two groups: only 19 per cent of the poor comprehenders' stories used the past tense, compared with 57 per cent of the skilled childrens' stories. We are not claiming that past tense is 'better': many talented writers use the present tense to great effect. But poor comprehenders tended to use just this tense, contributing to the list-like quality of their stories, while good comprehenders were more likely to vary the tense used to fit the demands of the story: predominantly past tense but with occasional uses of the present, perhaps for dramatic effect and immediacy.

We also looked at the way children referred to characters in the story: whether the references were appropriately varied and unambiguous (e.g. *the man saw the table . . . he went into the shop*) or whether they were either repetitious (e.g. *the man saw the table . . . the man went into the shop*) or ambiguous (e.g. *he saw the table . . . he went into the shop*, where the referent of 'he' has not been introduced). There was a tendency for skilled children to use the first pattern, which was smoother and clearer, more frequently than the less skilled children did. However, more interesting than this was the way that the children in the two groups were influenced by the conditions under which they told the story. For some of the stories, we presented the pictures one at a time, and the children did not know what would happen next. This makes it quite difficult to plan any coherent strategy for the use of referring expressions, because you do not know who is the main character or who will appear in the next picture. There was little difference between the two groups here: both used the repetitious or ambiguous style about half of the time. In a second condition, we showed the children all the pictures before they told the story. This gave them the opportunity to plan the best way of referring to the characters, for example using pronouns more often for the main character. This mode of presentation gave no advantage to the poor comprehenders: they carried on using the same style they had used in the other condition. But the good comprehenders could derive benefit from this condition: they used the more varied and appropriate pattern of reference for 83 per cent of the stories. The differences between the narratives of the two groups can be seen in these examples, from a poor comprehender, Tina, and a good one, Lucy, respectively:

> (TINA) A man and a lady is walking along and the doggie is behind them and there's some chicken hanging out of their bag and the dog bites it and they have a picnic and all the food is gone.

> (LUCY) Once there was a man and a lady and a dog and they went for a walk to have a picnic and they took two legs with them. When they came near the spot they were gonna have their picnic, the dog was trying to get their food because he thought the food was for him so he ate the food, and when they got to their picnic spot they looked in and everything was gone and they were so surprised they went home and got their dinner at home.

Lucy seems to have some general plan in mind, as she mentions the couple's intention to have a picnic, and their approach to the picnic spot, which only appears in the final picture of the sequence. This planning requires her to look ahead, and to modify the description of the current picture with respect to what will be said about subsequent ones. Tina merely describes one or two aspects of each picture, and seems to focus on each picture in isolation, to provide an external place-marker of where she is in the story. Also, notice that the central point of the story is not clear in Tina's story. There is no indication that the couple are surprised at the disappearance of the chicken, and it is not even clear why 'all the food has gone': without seeing the pictures, a listener might assume that the couple ate the food themselves.

These stories bring out a more general issue about how to tell a good story: you need to have an idea of the 'point' of the narrative, otherwise the story has no interest or purpose. We investigated children's understanding of story points in another story-narration study with 8–9-year-old children. After they had told a story from picture sequences, children were asked to choose, from four statements: 'What was the most important thing about the story, the point of it?' So, for example, in a story where a cowboy goes into a cowboy accessories shop, he pretends he wants to examine a lasso, and uses it to tie up the shopkeeper, and robs the till. We asked the children to choose one of the following four statements (adults were unanimous in choosing statement 1):

1  A cowboy tricks and robs the shopkeeper.
2  A cowboy buys a lasso.
3  A cowboy is in the shop.
4  A kind shopkeeper gives the cowboy some money.

Overall the skilled comprehenders picked the main point of the stories 79 per cent of the time, compared with only 46 per cent for the less-skilled comprehenders. It is clear that the good comprehenders are much better at understanding the main point of a story, and it is interesting that they are better at understanding the point of even picture sequences.

Some other work that is related to this issue has been done recently by Kate Cain at Sussex. She assessed how good and poor comprehenders understood the role of a title. The children were asked what a title could tell the reader about a story. If they seemed unsure, or did not respond, they were asked what a specific title might tell them about a story, e.g. 'Jack and the Beanstalk'. The children's responses were scored as correct if they said things like the title 'tells you what it's about', or gave an example such as: 'The Princess and the Pea – well, you can tell it's going to be about a princess and a pea'. Other responses, such as 'the words that are in the story' or 'whether it's good or not' were not allowed as correct. Overall, far more skilled than less-skilled comprehenders were able to produce an acceptable answer.

These findings indicate that less-skilled comprehenders have less clear ideas than skilled ones about how stories are typically structured – they tend to produce 'stories' that are less integrated and coherent than those of skilled comprehenders, and do not appreciate the main point of stories, even when the stories are presented as a series of pictures.

## Comprehension Monitoring

The third skill area we mentioned was that of comprehension monitoring. Some recent work in this area has shown that less-skilled comprehenders have difficulty in detecting problems of various kinds in short texts. Previous developmental studies, for instance by Ellen Markman,[5] have shown that young children generally have difficulty in saying explicitly what is wrong with a text so, in the experiments we report here, we used slightly older good and poor comprehenders (9–10 year olds).

In the first experiment (an undergraduate project, conducted by Deborah Samols), we explored both 'spontaneous' and 'directed' comprehension monitoring whilst the children were reading short passages which contained misspelt words and jumbled sentences. An example passage is shown below:

### Comprehension monitoring: example passage
### Fortune tellers

We all know about events in the past because we can remember them, but we do not know about the future in the same kind of way. The future is uncertain. It is for us to be sure impossible about what will happen.

There are people who say that they know what will take place in the future. Some of these people are called 'fortune tellers'. If you go to see them, they will tell you what they think will happen to you. For example, you might be told that you will be going on a long trep. You might be told that someone who seems to be a friend is really an enemy.

The fortune teller may perp into a crystal ball, where she says she can see pictures of the future. She may tell you that the pictures are incomplete or imperfect, so she can only give you clues. In this a better chance way she has of being right. The more detail she gives, the more likely she is to get it wrong.

To assess spontaneous monitoring, the children were simply asked to read aloud the passages, without any indication that anything was wrong. Their ability to detect the errors was assessed by monitoring their hesitations, repetitions and self-corrections as they read aloud. The children were also asked if they has noticed anything that did not make sense in the texts. We found no differences between the groups on the measures of spontaneous monitoring. However, 67 per cent of the good comprehenders reported noticing that parts of the passages did not make sense when asked if they had noticed anything unusual, whereas only 17 per cent of the less-skilled group reported doing so – a highly significant difference. Disappointingly, however, only one of the good comprehenders could identify the problematic lines in the texts. There were clear differences between the groups when they were told that some parts of the story might not make sense, and they were specifically requested to underline any words or sentences that they did not understand (directed monitoring). The numbers of problematic words and phrases as a proportion of the total numbers of words or phrases underlined was calculated. Surprisingly, even the good comprehenders were not very good at this task: only 51 per cent of their word underlinings and 56 per cent of their phrase underlinings were correct. However, these figures were markedly better than those for the less-skilled comprehenders: 17 per cent and 25 per cent respectively. Thus, there were large differences between the good and poor comprehenders in their ability to detect both problematic words and phrases. The children were also asked questions about the passages, after both the spontaneous and the directed conditions. Overall, the skilled comprehenders were better than the less-skilled comprehenders at answering questions. However, the directed condition did not lead to better performance on the comprehension questions in either group.

In a further study, comprehension monitoring was assessed using an inconsistency detection paradigm (similar to that used by Markman[5] for example). In this study, the children has to detect inconsistencies that depended on the integration of information between two sentences in the text. For example, they might read that 'Moles cannot see very well, but their hearing and sense of smell are good' and, later in the same passage, that 'Moles are easily able to find food for their young because their eyesight is so good'. The passage from which this example is taken is shown below.

### Inconsistency detection: example passage Moles
Moles are small brown animals and they live underground using networks of tunnels.

*Moles cannot see very well, but their hearing and sense of smell are good.*

They sleep in underground nests lined with grass, leaves and twigs.

Moles use their front feet for digging and their short fur allows them to move along their tunnels either forwards or backwards.

They mainly eat worms but they also eat insects and snails.

Moles are easily able to find food for their young because their eyesight is so good.

——This passage makes sense, it does not need to be changed.
——This passage does not make sense, it needs to be changed.

In this experiment, there was a further variable: the inconsistencies were either in adjacent sentences, or were separated by several sentences. Thus, for some children, the italicized sentence (which was not, of course, italicized in the texts shown to the children) appeared immediately prior to the final sentence of the passage. In this way, the memory load intrinsic to the task was manipulated. There were also a number of control passages, which did not contain inconsistencies, to ensure that the children were not trying to find problems where none existed. Once again, 9–10-year-old subjects were used in this experiment.

The children were asked to read the passages out loud, and to identify anything that 'didn't make sense'. They were given an example of a blatant inconsistency of the sort that they should be looking for. They were asked to read at their own pace, to underline any problems they found in the passage, and then to tick an overall assessment of the passage at the bottom of the page (as shown above). The children were also asked to explain any problems that they identified. If they did not identify a problem on the first reading, testing did not stop immediately. They were told that there was a problem in the passage, and they were asked to re-read the passage and try to identify it. If the child still failed to identify the inconsistency on the second reading, the experimenter underlined the two inconsistent sentences and asked if they made sense together. If a child was still unable to identify the problem at this stage, the experimenter turned to the next passage. The child was allocated a score of 0–3 for each passage, depending on whether or not they identified the inconsistency, and how much prompting they required before they could do so.

Thus, a maximum score was obtained if they marked the correct option at the end of the passage and were able to explain the inconsistency.

The results showed that the skilled comprehenders were better at detecting the inconsistencies overall (mean score 5.1 out of 6) than the less-skilled group (mean score 3.7). There was also an effect of the distance between the two inconsistent sentences: when the two sentences were adjacent, the task was much easier. However, the difference was much greater for the poor than for the good comprehenders – good comprehenders' performance was barely affected by whether the sentences were adjacent in the text, or were separated by several other sentences. The performance on the control passages (which did not contain any inconsistencies) was uniformly high in both groups. The performance on the inconsistent passages suggests that the integration of information across sentences in a passage is much more difficult for less-skilled than for skilled comprehenders. We (Yuill, Oakhill and Parkin[6]) found similar results with younger children in a task that required the detection of apparent anomalies in text. The less-skilled comprehenders could readily resolve anomalies in passages (e.g. a boy is *praised* by his mother for not sharing his sweets with his little brother) only if the apparent anomaly and the information that resolved it (in this case, that the little brother was on a diet) were in adjacent sentences. If the two items of information were separated by a few sentences, the less-skilled comprehenders could not seem to integrate them, and performed very poorly. These findings indicate that the performance of children on these tasks may be related to their ability to integrate information in working memory, and we will discuss this issue in the next section.

## Working Memory and Text Comprehension

Work with adults, by Meredyth Daneman and Patricia Carpenter,[7] has shown that a variety of comprehension skills are related to performance on a verbal working memory test in adults. These findings led us to assess working memory in our groups of good and poor comprehenders. The children who participated in the anomaly detection study outlined above also had their working memory assessed using a non-linguistic working memory test. In this test, the children were required to read out loud sets of three digits, and recall the final digits in each of the sets without looking back at them. So, for example, they might read the sets.

    9 - 4 - 1
    5 - 3 - 6
    2 - 7 - 8

and have to recall the final digits, 1, 6, 8, in order. The difficulty of the test was increased by increasing the number of sets of digits to be processed and thus the number of final digits to be recalled: the children had to recall either two, three or four digits. We found that the skilled and less-skilled comprehenders performed very similarly on the easiest version of the task, but that the less-skilled comprehenders were worse than the skilled ones on the two harder versions of the task. We have now replicated this pattern of findings many times.

Thus, one plausible reason for the problems of the less-skilled comprehenders might be that their poorer working memories are preventing them from efficient text processing, and limiting their ability to make inferences, integrate information and understand the overall structure of a text. However, other work of ours indicates that deficient working memory cannot provide a complete explanation for the less-skilled comprehenders' problems. For instance, some recent work by Kate Cain at Sussex has been looking into children's reading habits. She has been asking both children and their parents questions about the amount of reading they do at home, the numbers of books owned, and library membership and use. (This study differs from the recent work brought together by Keith Topping and Sheila Wolfendale,[8] which primarily addresses the effects of parents listening to their children read, or actively coaching them in reading, rather than literacy activities more broadly.) Although the numbers of participants in Cain's study are fairly small at the moment, some interesting findings are emerging. For instance, skilled comprehenders are *read to* significantly more frequently than less-skilled comprehenders. Similarly, more of the skilled than less-skilled comprehenders said they had visited a library, and more of their parents said they were members of a library, though the latter differences did not reach statistical significance. These findings may mean that the poorer comprehenders have not had the same level of exposure to stories and story structures from a very early age that skilled comprehenders might have had. Thus, they might have missed out on hundreds or even thousands of hours of story reading and book sharing from a very early age, and this experience, if it proves to be crucial to later reading comprehension skill, would be exceedingly difficult to compensate for (even if such compensation were found to be effective at a later age). Of course, it could be that poorer comprehenders are read to less *because* they are poor comprehenders, and perhaps do not enjoy being read to, or are not rewarding to read to. We end this chapter on a more optimistic note, because we have found that even relatively short-term training studies can be very effective in improving comprehension.

## Remediation Studies

There are three main ways in which comprehension of and learning from text might be improved, only one of which we consider in any detail here. First, additions and changes to the text could be made, to improve its comprehensibility and memorability. Additions might include pictures, subheadings and summaries; other changes might be to improve the organization or coherence of the text. These sorts of changes are ones that are made *for* readers, and do not require any effort on their part. Second, readers can be encouraged to engage in various activities either while they are reading or after reading a text, for example note-taking, underlining or summary-writing (such activities are often called 'study aids'). Research discussed by Oakhill and Garnham[9] has also shown that they can be used to improve comprehension. Third, children can be taught to apply processing strategies as they are reading: ways of thinking about the text, whether it relates to what they know, and whether their understanding is adequate. Such strategies differ from the first two types in that they rely on what is going on *in the reader's head*, rather than on external aids to comprehension. Most remediation studies have attempted to train children in such strategies on the assumption that it is most useful to develop procedures that can then be applied to any text.

The aim of the studies we describe in this section was to see if less-skilled readers' comprehension could be improved. The rationale was that, if less-skilled children can be trained in the skills they are supposed to lack, then their comprehension should improve. If the poor comprehenders' understanding is deficient *because* they lack the skills in which they are being trained, then we would expect that the less-skilled comprehenders might improve to the same level as the skilled ones following training, but the skilled ones would not benefit from training (since they already have the skills being trained).

The general idea of the first study (Yuill and Oakhill[10]) we will describe here was to try to make children more aware of, and get them more involved in, their own comprehension: to encourage inferencing and comprehension monitoring. As well as the group who received training (which we will come to in a moment), there were two 'control' groups, who spent the same amount of time with the experimenter but doing activities which we did not expect to improve their comprehension. All three groups spent a total of seven sessions of about thirty minutes each with the experimenter. One of the control groups simply spent their time answering questions about a series of short passages. The other group had training in rapid word decoding. As we mentioned earlier, one theory of poor comprehension suggests that *accurate* word recognition is not sufficient for efficient comprehension, but that words must also be recognized quickly and automatically. If they are not, then the resources devoted to word recognition will not be available for comprehension processes, which will suffer. This group read the same texts as the other group, and practised decoding lists of words from them. Thus, the improvement of the trained group could be compared with that of the control groups.

Like the control groups, the groups who received training were seen in seven separate sessions of about thirty minutes each. There were three components to the training. First, practice in *lexical inferences* was included in all seven sessions. Here, the children were encouraged to say what they could work out about a sentence or story from the individual words. For instance, in the sentence 'Sleepy Tom was late for school again', we can infer from 'sleepy' in that context that Tom has probably only just got up, and perhaps that he went to bed late, or habitually goes to bed late. The name 'Tom' suggests that Tom is a pupil, rather than a teacher, at the school because he is referred to by his first name, rather than being called 'Mr', and so on. The children were given practice in applying this technique, first with sentences, and then with short abstract stories of the sort shown below. Second, in four of the sessions, the children engaged in *question generation*. They were invited to generate questions such as 'Who was crying?' and 'Where was Billy?' for the passage shown (the questions listed were *not* presented in this training condition). The children took turns to generate questions. Third, in one session, they were encouraged to engage in *prediction*. In this session, part of the text was covered and the children were encouraged to guess at what was missing. After they had done so, the text was revealed and the appropriateness of their guesses was discussed with them.

The control group who did comprehension exercises were first told about the importance of accurate comprehension. The children in the group shared the reading of the text, and took turns at attempting to answer the set question on it. A sample text with questions is shown below.

### Inference training: example text

Billy was crying. His whole day was spoilt. All his work had been broken by the wave. His mother came to stop him crying. But she accidentally stepped on the only tower that was left. Billy cried even more. 'Never mind,' said his mother, 'We can always build another one tomorrow.' Billy stopped crying and went home for his tea.

EXAMPLE QUESTIONS (exercise group only)
Where was Billy?
Why was Billy crying?
What had the wave broken?
Why did his mother go to him?
Why did Billy cry even more?

*Table 6.3*  Inference training study: average improvement (months)

|              | Rapid decoding | Comprehension exercises | Inference training |
|--------------|----------------|-------------------------|--------------------|
| Less-skilled | 6.00           | 13.71                   | 17.38              |
| Skilled      | 10.33          | 5.43                    | 5.92               |

The children were given little feedback on their answers by the experimenter, except that obvious errors were corrected. However, the children often discussed the answers amongst themselves which, as we shall see later, may have influenced the results. The children in the other control group, who were given training in rapid decoding, practised reading words, including the most difficult words, from the same texts as quickly as possible.

After a period of about two months, during which the training took place, the children were re-tested on a different form of the Neale Analysis. The improvement scores for the six groups are shown in table 6.3. As can be seen, the very smallest increase in improvement was six months. However, the absolute differences in improvement mean very little because the different forms of the Neale Analysis may not be exactly parallel, or because the children just happen to make rapid progress in reading at the time of year the testing was done. What is remarkable, though, are the *relative* differences in improvement in the various groups. The less-skilled comprehenders benefited from inference training more than the skilled comprehenders,and the less-skilled group who received inference training improved more than those given decoding practice. However, the surprising aspect of these results, from our point of view, was that comprehension exercises also improved comprehension. Indeed, the improvement of the inference groups was not significantly different from those given comprehension exercises. Training did not differentially affect reading speed or accuracy of word decoding – there were no differences between the groups on these measures. The gains in comprehension scores after this relatively short period of training were impressive. However, it was surprising that the group given inference training did not improve more than those given comprehension exercises. One possible explanation for this result is that children in the latter group discussed their answers, and often argued with one another about what was the correct answer. These discussions may have had the effect of increasing their awareness of their comprehension. In addition, as can be seen from the example text, the texts used were rather abstract and obscure (to provide suitable material for the group given inference training) and this in itself may have encouraged more inferential processing and reflection than would have occurred with more traditional stories.

We have also explored, in collaboration with Sima Patel at Sussex, the effects of training in generating mental images of the events in a text on comprehension. Michael Pressley's work, for example,[11] has shown that imagery can be successful as a way of improving children's comprehension of stories, but it is not until about 8 that children can learn to use self-generated images. We explored whether less-skilled comprehenders might benefit from imagery training, and also addressed the issue of whether imagery might be particularly suitable for aiding memory for particular sorts of information (Oakhill and Patel[12]). We did this by asking the children three different sorts of question. The first type, 'factual' questions, tapped memory for facts that were explicit in the texts. The second type, 'inferential', asked about information that could only be inferred from the story, and the third, 'descriptive', asked about details that might be particularly likely to come to the reader's attention if an image had been formed. An example text, with the three types of question, is shown below.

### Imagery training study: example story and questions
The step ladder was put away safely behind the door which was just to the right of the cooker. The three shelves were up at last and, even with a sore thumb, Terry Butcher was happy. The hammer that had caused the pain was put away in the tool box with the other tools.

Linda, Terry's wife, came into the room with a box of crockery. 'The shelves are for my little model aeroplanes,' said Terry, in a stern voice. 'We'll see,' was the reply from Linda.

A little while later, when Terry was putting away the tool box, he heard a loud scream and the sound of breaking glass and china. Terry walked back into the room and was angry. 'I warned you about those shelves,' he said to Linda.

How many shelves had been put up? (factual)
Why did Terry have a sore thumb? (inferential)
Describe the scene in the room when Linda screamed
(descriptive)

We selected good and poor comprehenders with a mean age of
9.7. Each group was divided into two subgroups, one of which
was given training in imagery. The imagery training took place
in small groups (four or five children) over three sessions, on
different days. The children were told that they would be learning
to 'think in pictures' as they read stories, to help them to answer
questions about them. Nine stories were used altogether: four for
training, and five in the test session. In the first training session
the children read one of the stories, and the experimenter then
produced two drawings: one was a cartoon-like sequence of four
pictures, which represented the main sequence of events in the
story. The other was a single picture, which represented the main
event in the story. The children were shown how each of the
pictures related to the story, and were encouraged to use these
'pictures in their minds' to help them to answer questions about
the stories. For a second story in this session, the children were
not shown pictures but were encouraged to formulate their own
mental images. They discussed their pictures and received feedback and suggestions from the experimenter. In a second session,
a similar procedure was followed. In the final training session, the
children were not shown any drawings. The imagery procedure
was reiterated, and the children read and answered questions about
a new story and a discussion of their 'mental pictures' took place,
as in the first two sessions.

The children who did not receive imagery training saw the
same stories, also spread over three sessions. They read the stories
and answered the questions, and their answers were then discussed with them. The children in these groups spent as long
with the experimenter as those in the imagery training groups. In
the test phase, the groups who had received the imagery training
were reminded of this strategy before they read the test stories,
and were reminded to use their mental pictures to help them to
answer the questions. The children in the control condition were

told to read the stories very carefully and to answer the questions in as much detail as possible.

The results showed that, overall, the good comprehenders answered more questions correctly than poor ones, and that the children given imagery training performed better than the control group. As predicted, the poor comprehenders given imagery training showed a marked improvement in memory for the passages: they performed significantly better on the test questions than did the control group of poor comprehenders. There was no such difference between the groups of good comprehenders. Imagery training did not have a differential effect for the different types of questions: where there was improvement, it was general, and not related to particular question types. These results show that imagery training was especially beneficial for those children who do not possess adequate comprehension skills. Poor comprehenders may show a particular benefit from imagery training because it enables them, or forces them, to integrate information in the text in a way that they would not normally do. Of course, the finding that the comprehension of the good group did not improve with imagery does not necessarily mean that they already use imagery. It may be that they have some equally efficient strategy for remembering information from text, and that training in imagery gives them no additional advantage, Imagery may help poor comprehenders by giving them a strategy to help them to overcome some of the limitations on their comprehension skills. For instance, the ability to use imagery strategies may give poor comprehenders a way to help circumvent their memory limitations by enabling them to use a different, and perhaps more economical, means of representing information in the text.

In conclusion, we have shown that two very different types of training can have substantial effects on the comprehension scores of less-skilled comprehenders, at least in the short term. However, further work is needed to establish the long-term effects of such training. Although these findings give us cause for optimism, we conclude this section with two notes of caution. First, most methods of improving comprehension assume that poor comprehenders will benefit from being taught the skills that good readers use. However, the picture might not be so simple: the fact that poor readers lack some skills might indicate that, at least in some cases, they are unable to use them. Second, some forms of instruction might need to wait until after the beginning stages of learning to read, until decoding skills are fairly well established. A related point is that young readers may find learning to use skills such as imagery and comprehension monitoring very difficult – it is not until about 9, for instance, that children are typically able to understand and use imagery. Of course, these reservations about specific training in comprehension skills should not be taken to mean that reading for meaning should not be encouraged from the very beginning, but just that deliberate training of comprehension skills may need to be delayed.

## Conclusions

The general picture that emerges of less-skilled comprehenders is of children who are poor at making inferences and connecting up ideas in a text. Their problem seems not to be restricted to understanding the written word: in general they also have difficulties with listening comprehension and in understanding picture sequences. Working memory may play a part in such skills: our work has shown that less-skilled comprehenders perform poorly on a test of working memory. Such a deficit could readily explain the less-skilled comprehenders' problems in making inferences, understanding story structure and monitoring their comprehension. However, patterns of causality have yet to be established. In any case, this seems very unlikely to be a complete explanation of the less-skilled children's problem, since inference skills can be trained, and one would not expect working memory to be susceptible to training. One possibility that reconciles these two sets of findings is that less-skilled comprehenders do have a basic deficit in working memory which affects their comprehension, but that they can be taught strategies that help them to circumvent their memory limitations. In addition, some findings are emerging to show that extensive experience of being read to may be important. It may be that being read to from an early age turns out to be a crucial factor in the development of comprehension skills.

NOTES

1 Perfetti, C.A. 1985: *Reading Ability*, Oxford: Oxford University Press.
2 Yuill, N.M. and Oakhill, J.V. 1991: *Children's Problems in Text Comprehension: An Experimental Investigation*, Cambridge: Cambridge University Press.
3 Bishop, D. 1983: *Test for Reception of Grammar*, Manchester: Department of Psychology, University of Manchester.
4 Oakhill, J.V. 1984: 'Inferential and memory skills in children's comprehension of stories', *British Journal of Educational Psychology*, 54, 31–9
5 Markman, E. 1977: 'Realizing that you don't understand: a preliminary investigation', *Child Development*, 48, 986–92.
6 Yuill, N.M., Oakhill, J.V. and Parkin, A.J. 1989: 'Working memory, comprehension ability and the resolution of text anomaly', *British Journal of Psychology*, 80, 351–61.
7 Daneman, M. and Carpenter, P. 1980: 'Individual differences in working memory and reading', *Journal of Verbal Learning and Verbal Behavior*, 19, 450–66.
8 Topping, K. and Wolfendale, S. (eds) 1985: *Parental Involvement in Children's Reading*, London: Croom Helm.
9 Oakhill, J.V. and Garnham, A. 1988: *Becoming a Skilled Reader*, Oxford: Blackwell.
10 Yuill, N.M. and Oakhill, J.V. 1988: 'Effects of inference awareness training on poor reading comprehension', *Applied Cognitive Psychology*, 2, 33–45.
11 Pressley, G.M. 1976: 'Mental imagery helps eight-year-olds remember what they read', *Journal of Educational Psychology*, 68, 355–9.
12 Oakhill, J.V. and Patel, S. 1991: 'Can imagery training help children who have comprehension problems?', *Journal of Research in Reading*, 14, 106–15.

# Postscript

## Elaine Funnell and Morag Stuart

This book has mapped out some well-trodden paths through a number of controversies about reading processes and the process of learning to read. These paths have taken us through discussions about methods of teaching reading (the real books, the apprenticeship approach, psycholinguistic guessing games); through reading processes and the part they play in learning to read (phonological awareness and word recognition skills, and how they relate to teaching methods); through techniques of assessing reading competence and improving poor reading; and, finally, through the role of language comprehension in reading.

The paths are well trodden because they have attracted considerable attention in the fields of education and experimental psychology over recent years and, as a result of many joint endeavours, have begun to converge to form a convincing body of evidence.

However, we should not wish to leave you in the belief that this is all that needs to be known and understood about reading development. Research approaches have their fads, just as educational practices do, and the current emphasis on phonological aspects of reading, important though it is, may well have drawn attention away from the need to understand and explain other aspects of reading too. How are the visual patterns of familiar words remembered? Why do some children, with good phonological skills, fail to develop a good memory for the visual forms of what should be familiar written words? How does the level of spoken language of a child affect the ability to learn to read? What role does short-term memory play? These are just some of the broader questions that are either attracting less attention at present or have not been included in this book.

We should also be most concerned if the current theoretical emphasis on the importance of phonology in learning to read, which has been addressed in this book, was misinterpreted to imply that the teaching of phonics in the classroom should be emphasized to the detriment of other teaching methods. This is not the intended message of this book. Quite the reverse. The evidence suggests that a variety of teaching methods is required to develop the full range of reading processes that have been shown to be available to the skilled reader, and dependence upon one method only is likely to develop some processes but not others.

The message we should like to leave you with is that experimental research into reading is exciting and rewarding, both to the experimental psychologist, the teacher and the educationalist, and that it can be carried out successfully in the classroom, preferably through the happy collaboration of all concerned, including, of course, the children.

# Index